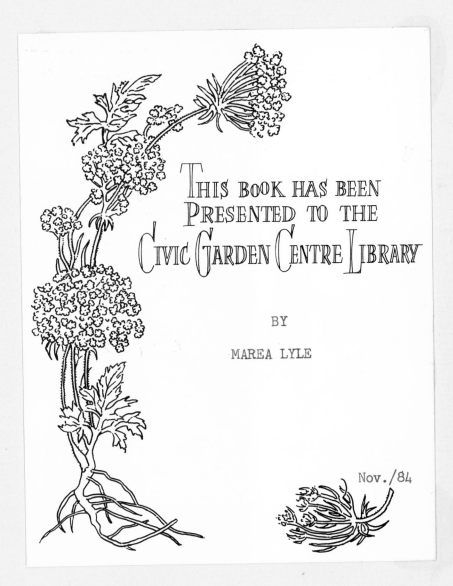

THIS BOOK HAS BEEN
PRESENTED TO THE
CIVIC GARDEN CENTRE LIBRARY

BY

MAREA LYLE

Nov./84

MODERN
FLOWER
ARRANGING

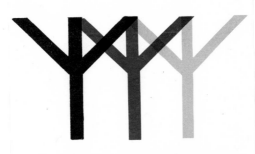

**Civic Garden Centre
Library**

MODERN FLOWER ARRANGING

Edith Brack

B. T. BATSFORD LTD. LONDON

For Alan

**My special thanks to Cyril Lindley and my husband
for their skilful photography**

By the same author:
Flower Arrangement: Free-Style

© Edith Brack 1982

First published in 1982

ISBN 0 7134 3893 2

Filmset in Monophoto Baskerville by
Latimer Trend & Company Ltd, Plymouth
and printed in Great Britain by
The Anchor Press Ltd,
Tiptree, Essex

for the publishers
B. T. Batsford Ltd.
4 Fitzhardinge Street
London W1H 0AH

Contents

Introduction (vi)

Introduction

This book sets out to illustrate the point that flower arranging is not an expensive hobby. There are those who do not even attempt it because they think it cannot be done without using masses of expensive flowers and foliage. But some highly original designs can easily be made with a minimum of materials, so do not be intimidated— have a go!

Changing styles in interior decoration in the past have led to changing styles in flower arrangement and it is natural that new styles will evolve with each new age. Modern flower arranging as we know it today has been largely influenced by *Ikebana* (Japanese flower arranging) where the use of space and the beauty of individual flowers play such an important part.

Simplicity is the Ikebana watchword and so it is with me. The word itself suggests ease of execution, although simplicity is not always easy to achieve. But therein lies the challenge. You will find it far more interesting to arrange flowers in the modern manner where self-expression counts than to arrange them *en masse* with little or no forethought. It gives more reign to one's ingenuity and is much more stimulating.

The clean, uncluttered rooms which are a feature of many homes today lend themselves particularly well to this type of flower arranging as do offices and modern churches. Even in the more traditional setting they can make a compatible feature provided the background is fairly plain.

In the four sections of this book I have included suggestions for both suitable flowers and foliage to grow for your arrangements. Even if you only have a small garden try to find something unusual to grow which will give your designs that extra something which will lift them above the ordinary into the extraordinary class.

Just as arrangements in the modern manner are economical in materials containers need not be expensive either. A good look round the house will probably provide you with some suitable ones. Keep an open mind when searching as many things bought for other purposes often make excellent containers, although these days it is much easier to buy them specifically made for modern arrangements. When I started looking for containers there were not many about and remembering a good flower arranging maxim—'if you can't buy them make them'—I became a potter and began to make my own. Now, fifteen years later, I have a sizeable collection of original containers of which many have been used in this book.

Flower arranging has many spin-offs and pottery making is one I would whole-heartedly recommend. Another is the enjoyment obtained from the constant search for 'found objects' like driftwood, stones, shells and other interesting items, both natural and man-made. It makes country walks and beachcombing far more interesting when, to add to the pleasure of the day itself, you bring home a permanent reminder to use in your designs.

Finally, I would add that long after the mass arrangements have been forgotten you will find that some simple design which has captured your imagination will stay in your mind for ever.

SPRING

SPRING is my favourite time of the year. I get the same feeling of joy each year when I see the trees coming into leaf and all the fresh new growth in the garden. The sun has only to shine and I'm on top of the world.

Spring flowers, however, are not the easiest to arrange—especially in the modern manner. They seem far more at home in a naturalistic setting than do flowers which come out later in the year. Nevertheless, when they are arranged successfully in a modern design the individual beauty of the flowers is much more apparent than when they are arranged in the mass.

In this type of arrangement a pin-holder alone is used to anchor the material in a shallow container and this is an advantage. Spring flowers generally last better in about an inch or two of water. They do not like being pushed into floral foam which tends to clog their stems and hinder the intake of water.

This tall oblong container has two such shallow compartments for flowers with one at the top and the other at the base. It is a slab-built pot made by rolling out the clay like pastry and then cutting out the pieces from a template to one's own design. The individual pieces are then welded together before it is biscuit fired and finally glazed. I have two such containers; one is dark bronzy-green and this, a smaller pale green one.

The idea for this design came on a not-so-sunny spring day when there had been a last-gasp flurry of winter snow. The trees stood out against the sky in silhouette with the snow delineating their branches. To give this impression I cut two pieces of lilac with its ideal skeletal branches and placed them in the upper compartment of the container. The first piece was anchored on to a pin-holder while the second piece was hooked upside down on to the first at a convenient twig. Two daffodils with their leaves were placed in the lower opening at the side to suggest their emergence from the undergrowth. A quick spray with artificial snow completed my interpretation of that view from my window.

This kind of design could equally well have been done with the corkscrew willow, *Salix matsudana* 'Tortuosa'. It has a wonderful outline which is seen at its best before it comes into leaf. In fact when it is cut the leaves shrivel up very quickly so this is much the better way to use it. This willow, like many of the same species, is simplicity itself to grow from cuttings. Just insert them in some damp soil—and stand back!

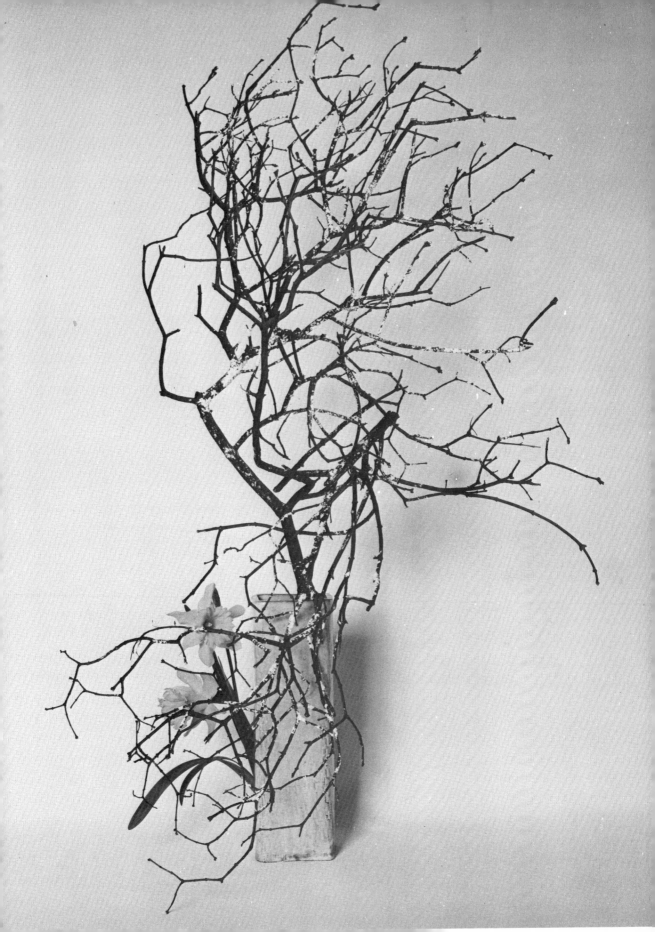

When winter seems never-ending and you yearn for the arrival of spring with all its exciting prospects why not take matters into your own hands and coax a few twigs and branches into early leaf? There are many accommodating trees and shrubs which lend themselves to a little gentle persuasion.

Cut the branches in mildish weather when they are full of sap, and preferably after rain. You will easily be able to recognize the right ones to choose as the buds will appear plump and full of promise. Scrape a couple of inches of bark from the bottom of the branches and then slit the stems up the centre with a crosscut to enable the water to be taken up readily. Place the branches in buckets of warm water and stand them in a warm place to open up. This can take anything from one to five weeks depending on the variety of plant chosen and the time of cutting.

Here are some possibles for you to try: *Chaenomeles* (Japanese quince), *Corylus* (hazel), *Forsythia, Fothergilla, Hammamelis mollis* (witch hazel), *Lonicera* (honeysuckle), *Magnolia, Malus* (crab apple), *Philadelphus* (mock orange), *Prunus* (flowering fruit trees), *Ribes* (flowering currant), *Salix* (willow), *Syringa* (lilac) and *Wisteria*. This list is by no means comprehensive and there are many others which yield to the treatment.

The flowering currant (*Ribes sanguineum*) used in this design was not forced but cut from the garden as I wanted its bright pink flowers. If it had been forced they would have been much paler, almost white. However, I wanted the pink to match the *Bergenia* flowers which are the highlight of the arrangement. The pot I have used has been left in its natural terra-cotta state and only the inside glazed to make it non-porous. The base, although it is a bought one, could easily be made with similarly cut pieces of bamboo fastened together with a leather thong. I have several of them and find them most useful to give extra visual weight when a container needs a little more emphasis.

The *Bergenia* (popularly known as 'elephant's ears') is a 'must' for flower arrangers. It can supply you with those heart-shaped or rounded fleshy leaves for all the twelve months of the year and I treat the flowers as an added bonus, coming as they do when flowers are scarce. *B. cordifolia* is possibly the commonest variety grown and you can never be sure what colour or colours its leaves will be when they die off. Mine usually remain green to the end but luckier friends boast of leaves with attractive tones of pink and red and sometimes even yellow.

The 'Springbok rakes' outline of this design might cause a raised eyebrow to a few who have never come across them before. They are in fact the stems of palmetto palm leaves which are commonly used in Malaysia for making fans but which have been cut into two, skeletonized, and painted shiny black. Many years ago when train fares were cheaper, I used to visit *Ikebana* exhibitions and demonstrations in London and these stems were won in a raffle after one of the demonstrations. You can imagine the funny looks I got from other passengers in the tube and on the main-line train when I carried them home unwrapped. They seem to be something of a rarity and so far I have not seen any others for sale, only photographs of them used in other flower arrangements.

The stems are very hard indeed and it is difficult to impale them on a pin-holder so I filled up the container with sand to just below the funnel and topped it up with water to the brim. This enabled me to plunge the stalks into the compacted sand at the angles I desired. The same idea can solve many problems which you may experience when using any tall container, whether narrow or with a splayed-out top. Alternatively, a pin-holder placed on the top of the sand will hold your stems satisfactorily. Instead of sand some arrangers use floral foam which has seen better days. Personally, I prefer the sand method as it is far more reliable.

Of course, you can use this idea with one of those irresistible Swedish glass containers. In this case it can be filled with plain glass marbles and the stems can then be easily threaded through them for safe anchorage. Another idea worth trying on a suitably shaped container is to make an open lattice top with Sellotape when the flowers can be arranged in the openings so provided. Some stemmed glass containers, such as large brandy glasses, are better reversed when a small container can then be placed on the base of the stem and the flowers arranged that way.

As with all aspects of flower arranging it is always well worthwhile experimenting with new ideas yourself. And you will experience a real thrill of satisfaction when you find a simple solution to a vexing problem.

The container for this design is from my new shiny black set which seems an ideal choice for use with such outline material. Just one piece of bright yellow forsythia bursting with flowers gave me the colourful impact I was looking for.

I am always saying what squirrels we flower arrangers are for hoarding all manner of things. This old cane basket, meant to be slipped on the wrist for a ball of wool when knitting, was rescued from going up in smoke one day whilst I was visiting a spring-cleaning friend of mine. I knew it would come in handy some time although not for its original purpose.

Basket-work such as this seems to lend itself so well for use with flowers. It must be one of the oldest crafts, derived no doubt from early man watching the birds weave their nests! The first baskets were probably made for storing and transporting grain and gradually over the years they were developed for all kinds of purposes and made from all kinds of materials. Today we even have some made purely for decorative purposes.

Good proportions and simple design are the things to look for when selecting a basket for flower arranging. It is true that baskets are generally considered rather informal, with a somewhat rustic air, but there are the more sophisticated Italian ones made with Milanese straw so that common-or-garden flowers as well as exotics can be used with them; and because baskets are usually neutral they are suitable for practically any colour scheme.

The Japanese have always used baskets of all kinds in their designs. Their well-known *Morimono* arrangements of fruit, vegetables and flowers are often made on flat basket trays which always look just right for the purpose. When they use a basket with a handle it must always be arranged so that it can be picked up by it and carried from place to place, which is an idea most Westerners now follow.

As you will no doubt realize, in all these designs using basketry a small receptacle to hold water will have to be concealed somewhere. In modern arrangements, the smaller the better is always the case, just as long as it will hold sufficient water for the flowers' needs. Times without number I have seen such arrangements ruined because the arranger has used a larger than necessary piece of floral foam. It all had to be hidden from view involving the use of additional materials and in the process the outlines of the designs were completely ruined.

Here I have placed the cane holder on a matt black wooden base and firmly secured it with Plasticine. This not only stabilizes the container but gives the arrangement its proper proportions. A small well-type pin-holder has been placed in the left segment and an interesting outline made from some beautifully curved common green ivy. Just one bunch of some bright yellow jonquil narcissus (called 'Sols', my florist assures me) has been added to give the necessary highlight.

I can't think of another flower which shows as much temperament as a tulip. It's as though it thinks it can improve on the way it has been arranged. One has only to turn one's back and there they are doing their own thing. They perversely twist in the opposite direction or even sometimes stand up straight when they have been arranged especially to show off their elegant curves. Not only that, 24 hours later you might even find that they have actually grown another inch or so!

Nevertheless, they are beautiful flowers when seen *en masse* in the garden or individually in an arrangement. And what a marvellous choice there is these days, in all colours, shapes and sizes! I particularly like the peony-flowered doubles, the graceful lily-flowering types and the fascinating parrot and fringed varieties. I grew some of the latter a few years ago and their heads were as big as ostrich eggs. When they were caught by some high winds they all broke off with about three inches of stem—and making use of 15 or 20 of them all at once was a challenge for any arranger, I can assure you.

The tulips I have used in this design are the popular mauve variety which florists seem to favour most and the silvery-green moon seemed an excellent choice for a container to go with them. It is not pottery this time but one which I made from hardboard and a strip of linoleum. The shapes were cut with a band-saw by 'the little man down the road'. A long strip of thick industrial lino was then cut, its length being the circumference of the outside edge, starting at an inch and opening out to two inches and tapering back to an inch. This was then glued with an impact adhesive to the hardboard and left for a couple of days. The outside was then covered with an anaglypta paper and finally sprayed with one of those useful motorcar touch-up aerosol paints. This container is not, of course, waterproof but it is a simple matter to pop a pot inside to hold the water. Another one I have has been very successfully covered with beaten sheet pewter. There are endless possibilities for coverings of all kinds and the beauty is that when you tire of them they can easily be changed.

Six tulips graduated in size follow the line of the container and a few pieces of dark green *chamaecyparis* have been added for contrast in colour and shape to the pale green tulip foliage. A couple of those large and lovely clematis flowers would look equally attractive in such a setting.

Plants which can withstand even the hardiest of winters are certainly a blessing to flower arrangers. The *Iris foetidissima* with its dark green glossy leaves is one. As well as its hardiness it has another desirable attribute in that it grows well in the shade. Its flowers are rather insignificant and a good thing, too, or we might be tempted to cut them and so miss their eye-catching fruits. For the plant's real beauty lies in its seed pods which split open and peel back to reveal clusters of scarlet berries in the autumn. It is well worth cutting a few and hanging them up to dry for use with your winter arrangements. If you paint the berries with colourless nail-varnish they are less likely to shrivel up and fall out of the pods as they would otherwise do.

Another iris equally worth growing but somewhat harder to get hold of is the *I. ochroleuca*. Its extra-long leaves—three feet or more—have an attractive twist in them and although they are not evergreen still manage to survive in milder winters. I have a splendid clump of them in the garden which provides a succession of flowers in late June. With their creamy-white standards and yellow-blotched falls they make an impressive sight.

Talking of impressive sights, there could be none finer than that of the yellow-striped sword-like foliage of the *I. pseudacorus* 'Variegata' in late May and early June. Although it will grow in the border it is far happier with its feet in water at the edge of a pond. What a pity it is that the stripes gradually fade away after it has flowered.

I feel that the iris is displayed at its best in a simple design but, as I said, the *foetidissima* flowers are not worthy of their attractive leaves so I have 'borrowed' the flowers of the Dutch iris which, as it happens, has rather unattractive foliage. An interchange of flowers and leaves like this where the one does no credit to the other is always worth considering.

The low blue bowl I have used matches exactly the colour of the iris and to carry through the colour scheme I have used blue-painted pebbles to hide the pin-holder.

Although these iris leaves will last long enough for you to replenish the flowers a couple of times they will eventually begin to die back from their tips. It is a good idea to take them out of water but leave them on the pin-holder to dry as they stand. You will find they will become a lovely biscuit colour and still retain the curves which you have already persuaded them to take. They would then make an excellent outline to use with a couple of bronze chrysanthemums in the autumn.

The Germans call it *Geweihholz* which means 'antler wood' and there could be no better description of the outline material I have used in this arrangement. It is a freak of nature which botanists call 'fasciated'. It is fairly rare and is coveted by flower arrangers. Although quite difficult to get hold of, especially the more curvaceous pieces, it is sometimes available at the more enterprising florists and you may find it on sale at the large flower and horticultural shows. I have also seen it on flower club sales tables where it is soon snatched up by enthusiastic members.

The reason for its fasciation—the abnormal growing together of two or more stems—is not really understood though in some cases it appears to be an inherited feature and in others it is the result of injury to the growing tip of the plant.

For all that it is an uncommon occurrence in most shrubs and plants, one of the willow family—the *Salix gladulosa* 'Setsuka'—can always be relied upon to throw up some fasciated stems and it is invariably spoken of as the 'fasciated willow'. You will also occasionally see a fusion of stem in tulips and hyacinths and I have even come across it in the garden in delphiniums.

It is hard to believe that the outline of this design is made with just one piece of the fasciated forsythia. However, I had to make one slight alteration to its original form by taking off the fan-shaped curved piece now at the mid-left position which was originally lower down on the right. It protruded at an angle which spoilt the overall outline. Don't be afraid to improve on nature with a bit of judicious pruning. But do consider it for a long time before you take action or you might later regret your impetuosity.

The pink tulips which I have used had such attractive centres that I have opened them out to show them off and at the same time given them a greater impact than they would have had if they had been left closed. It is quite easy to stroke the petals back gently using the thumb and first finger. This can only be successfully done with mature flowers otherwise they pop back into place almost immediately. I have grouped the flowers at the base of the wood so as not to hide its intriguing form.

The slab-built container is greenish-bronze, a colour which was obtained by spraying it with a mixture of copper and iron oxides before glazing: an ideal shade to enhance further the colour of the tulips.

This outline and container both make a marvellous foil for many flowers. It would look most effective with two or three garden roses in the summer or alternatively with a few medium-sized chrysanthemums in the autumn.

I've heard of rose shows, dahlia shows, sweet pea shows and chrysanthemum shows but never have I heard of a show devoted to the hyacinth yet, I read recently, back in the eighteen hundreds they were very popular. The very thought of walking into a hall chock-a-block with these flowers makes the mind boggle. While the sight would undoubtedly be magnificent the perfume must have been over-powering. Mind you, it is for their fragrance that I like them in the house.

These days, of course, through the wonders of science we can buy hyacinth bulbs which defy the laws of nature and come into flower over the Christmas period. These, I understand, are treated in special temperature and humidity controlled chambers to advance and develop to perfection the embryo flower bud which already exists within the bulb. However, I like to see them growing best of all in a low garden wall setting which we have in the garden. The wall was made to a height of 12 inches with broken pieces of flag stones left over when we made a paved area. It extends for about 10 feet and is enclosed at either end. A section about 12 inches wide runs down the centre. This was prepared for planting by putting a layer of crocks at the bottom which was then covered with a layer of peat and finally filled with compost. It is ideal for showing off flowers such as these and white hyacinths such as 'L'Innocence', 'Blizzard' and 'Carnegie' are my favourites. A good primrose-yellow one is 'City of Haarlem' and for a lovely ice-pink flushed with rose try 'Princess Margaret'. A good pastel blue and a popular choice is 'Queen of the Blues' but if you prefer a rich indigo-blue then 'King of the Blues' should appeal.

The two hyacinths I have used in this design are florists' flowers as I can't bring myself to cut those growing in the garden. They are pink in colour and go well with the two pieces of glaucous pine used for the outline. As I mentioned earlier, like most spring flowers, they dislike being arranged in floral foam but before you impale them on the pin-holder insert either wire or cocktail sticks up their stems. As the stems are soft and flaccid and the heads heavy you will have problems if you don't take these precautions.

The container I have used is an old favourite of mine inspired by a Japanese-type pot. It is slab-built, made in two main sections. First of all, the five leather-hard pieces of clay were joined together to make the oblong top piece. Then the three pieces were assembled to make the lower section, and when it had dried hard enough to support its own weight the upper and lower sections were joined. This means that for a pot such as this 12 separate pieces in all have to be welded together: quite a time-consuming exercise compared with the throwing of a pot on the wheel which can be done in a matter of minutes.

If, for some reason, I were only allowed to have three containers in my collection instead of the hundred-plus which I have, this one would be on the short-list. It is Japanese-inspired and I made it many years ago when I first began pottery. In fact, it was my inability to buy the sort of container I wanted for my *Ikebana* arrangements that started me off on this very exciting new hobby. Fortunately for arrangers there are now a number of potters about who specialize in this type of thing but 15 years ago when I started they did not seem to exist.

This pot was made before I had an electric wheel and I therefore had to use the slab-building method of construction. For this the clay is rolled out rather like pastry and then fashioned into the required shape. For this particular container I wrapped the clay round a cylinder core which had newspaper wrapped around the outside. When the clay had dried sufficiently to hold its shape I was able to slip it off quite easily. Two round discs had been cut out and put aside when the initial rolling was done, one for the base and the other to insert two inches down inside the cylinder. This gave me a two-tiered container.

This particular pot is glazed a celadon-green and is especially lovely to use with spring flowers. As it has been such a favourite of mine I have since made identical ones in terra-cotta, dark brown and black.

This is the kind of pot no flower arranger should be without as you do not seem to be able to do a poor arrangement in it. Even when you have shortish branches to use which would be out-of-scale with a low-type container the height of the pot solves this problem for you. And as the pot has a placement for flowers at the base the design never seems to be top-heavy. It lends itself well to being draped around with driftwood or it can be stood behind a larger dramatic piece where it may be completely hidden but able to provide a high and low placement for your flowers. I hope I have now justified my earlier remarks about this container being a must for all 'modern' arrangers!

The sight of forsythia in bloom on a sunny spring day certainly gladdens the heart and makes you think of summer days to come. The one used in this arrangement is *Forsythia* × *intermedia* but I find the long sweeping branches of the *F. suspensa* more attractive in many ways. With only five daffodils and two pieces of forsythia this is a very economical design but nevertheless one which is a true evocation of Spring. For many people the only way to display daffodils is in the naturalistic manner on a sliver of wood but I am sure you will agree they still look right used in this more modern interpretation.

Cherry blossom is the national flower of Japan and each year when it is at its zenith the public go to enormous lengths, even staying off work, to view it. From the end of March to early April the newspapers carry a chart called *sakura-zensen*, 'the cherry blossom front'. This gives the places and predicted day of the month which will be best for cherry blossom viewing. As the best time is short, only a week, it must be a nail-biting exercise for those making the forecasts. A strong wind or heavy rain could easily make liars of them all!

I can well understand this fixation of theirs. Seen *en masse* the beauty of cherry blossom is breath-taking, especially so in the moonlight when it takes on an ethereal quality. It is a great pity it has such a short flowering period. Whenever it is in blossom it seems to be a signal for the winds to blow and roads and gardens are soon strewn with pink confetti before we have even had time to enjoy it.

One of the most popular varieties is *Prunus* 'Kanzan', the one featured in this arrangement. It is a vigorous tree and is often seen growing in small gardens where it quickly gets out of hand. The *P.* 'Amanogara' is far more suitable for such a situation as it is a tree of erect columnar habit. Dense clusters of their semi-double, slightly scented, soft, pink flowers make it an eye-catching sight.

When cutting any type of blossom for an arrangement care should be taken to choose one of an interesting shape. Sometimes it will have to be pruned judiciously so that its beauty of line is more apparent. Many blossoms are hidden by their leaves so trim some of these off too. Not only will this improve the beauty of the branch but it will make the flowers last longer as it will prevent transpiration through the leaves.

For this design I chose a heavy U-shaped container of dark peacock-blue. The left side was packed with floral foam to facilitate easy anchorage of the trimmed piece of cherry blossom, with its double pink flowers and coppery-red foliage. A large and beautifully textured piece of dark driftwood has been hooked on to the container to give it extra visual weight and so improve its proportions.

This is a coil-built pot. The technique for its construction is both simple and basic whereby shapes are built up from long, even sausages of clay. These are placed one on top of the other and welded together with liquid clay (slip) and finally refined (fettled). This system is ideal for the more unconventional containers which cannot be thrown on the wheel or made by the slab-method. It is possible, however, to employ two or more of these methods on one particular piece, depending on its design.

Because of their sculptural qualities arum lilies (*Zantedeschia aethiopica*) are ideal for modern arrangements. I only possess two pots of them which are grown in the greenhouse but each year they regularly oblige with plenty of flowers for my arrangements. They are well worth growing and require little attention for the reward they give with their splendid flowers. Mine are in 10-inch pots in John Innes compost No. 2 but they can equally well be grown in a proprietary peat compost. Cover the rhizomes with 2–3 inches of soil and water immediately after planting, keeping the pots just moist until growth appears when they need watering moderately. Gradually increase the amount given until they are in full leaf when they require copious watering. I also feed mine at weekly intervals with a liquid fertilizer. When flowering is over I put the pots on their sides in the garden to dry off. In late September I bring them back into the greenhouse and pot them up in fresh soil for the cycle to start all over again.

They can be grown out of doors in the south and even in my area of the north-west they should survive if planted in a sheltered spot and given some extra protection for the winter.

This species can also be grown as a water plant and 'Crowborough' is a good form to choose for this purpose. Grown as an aquatic in 6–12 inches of water it will usually survive in most districts.

Two other varieties which you might like to try are *Z. elliottiana*, which is yellow, and *Z. rehmannii* which ranges from pink through to wine-red. Although I have had a first flowering of both I must confess that I have not been very successful thereafter with either. Incidentally, both of these require a higher minimum winter temperature than the easier-going arum.

The shiny black container is a coiled pot of mine. After a lot of experimentation I have recently discovered just what oxides to mix to obtain this japan-black finish so naturally I have exploited my good fortune to the full by making a set of containers of different shapes, all with the same glaze. This tall, waisted container was made in three sections before being joined together to give two separate compartments for holding water. It was then incised with vertical lines to give an interesting texture.

The twisted piece of black wood fits neatly over the top section into which I have put an arum lily with one of its leaves whilst another lily has been placed in the lower one.

The oatmeal and tan-flecked container used in this arrangement is made up from a set of six pieces which I made and glazed all at the same time so that there would be no colour variation when they were fired in the kiln. They can all be used separately or in any permutation of the set to give a varied choice. In fact, I seem to find a fresh variation every time I bring them into use and I regard them as among my happiest 'inventions'.

For this design I stood one of the D-shaped containers with its straight side to the front on one of the similarly-shaped bases and to make sure it was quite secure I fastened it with a fixative. Two pin-holders were placed inside, one on the left and one to the right, as the idea for my design consisted of two separate placements with space between. Trimmed *Edgeworthia* 'Mitsumata' gives the skeletal outlines and the flowers have been grouped together at the base of each. The flowers are the *Narcissi* 'Geranium', a Poetaz hybrid which bears three to five of these cream flowers with a bright orange cup on strong stems.

I look forward to the arrival of daffodils and narcissi each spring as a harbinger of sunny days ahead. And what an astonishing selection there is to choose from, although the lists of species and varieties are rather baffling. The Royal Horticultural Society has grouped narcissi into eleven divisions. The RHS Classified List and International Register contains no less than 8000 named cultivated varieties. Most of them have been raised in the last hundred years and the number is still being added to yearly.

When choosing some for the garden it is a good idea to go for those that cannot be bought at the florist. Here are a few suggestions: 'Thalia' with two or three flowers per stem of pale cream reflexed, back-swept petals and white cup; 'Dolly Mollinger' with broad, rounded, milk-white petals with a ruffled, almost double, crown of creamy orange; 'Lemon Beauty' which has creamy petals with a bold deep primrose line on each centre petal; 'Salome' with pure white petals and a salmon-rose trumpet, and the lime-yellow 'Spellbinder' with a trumpet which becomes nearly white as the flower ages.

Spring flowers do not last as long indoors as the summer and autumn ones. No doubt they prefer the cool of the garden to the dry atmosphere of our homes. Nevertheless, it is always worthwhile taking trouble to condition them correctly. If bought from the flower shop always re-cut the stem before placing them in about two inches of tepid water. Because of the cellular structure of bulb flowers it is not advisable to stand them in deep water otherwise the stems will become soggy and difficult to arrange.

The clematis, whose flowers range from the delicate to the flamboyant, is as useful as it is decorative. Whether you choose to have it clothing a fence, scrambling over a dead tree trunk, framing an archway or pergola, hiding an unsightly shed or climbing up into some tall tree it will be a joy forever. It will flower from April to November depending on the species and variety and it is easy to grow—provided the dreaded *wilt* does not get it. This sometimes strikes a healthy plant quite suddenly and reduces it to a miserable, wilted stalk. It is caused by a fungus but all is not lost; if the plant is cut back at the base, more often than not, it will shoot again from the root.

Even when you think there is not space for another single flower or shrub in the garden there is always room for a clematis. It only requires a toe-hold and it will soon find its own place in the sun as long as there is something for its twining leaf stalks to get hold of. It is a good idea to shade the base of the stem in some way either by low-growing plants or by a couple of pieces of broken paving stone. Now that these plants are usually bought in containers they can be planted at virtually any time. And once you have them others can easily be grown from their cuttings or by layering.

For covering the side of a house or garage you cannot beat *C. montana*. It is a vigorous species and in three years can race up a wall 30 feet high with a spread of 20 feet as it has done at the rear of our house. I planted a white one along with *C*. 'Tetra-rose', the larger lilac-pink variety with the bronze foliage, and the two intermingled make a breath-taking sight when they flower in May. I also have the ever-popular 'Nelly Moser', a pale mauve with a pink stripe which usually flowers in May and again in October and in a mild winter I have even had flowers at Christmas.

Some of the more popular hybrids with their colouring and flowering times are— 'Lasurstern', a clear blue which flowers from June to October; 'Ernest Markham', a glowing red in flower from July to October; 'Bee's Jubilee', a pink with carmine stripes—May to October; 'Marie Boisselot', a large pure white—June to August; 'Vyvyan Pennell', an exotic double-flowered violet-purple flushed with carmine—May to November and the popular 'Jackmanii Superba', dark violet-purple, flowering from July to October. The *C. tangutica* is a favourite with flower arrangers, not for its tiny yellow Chinese lantern flowers but for its fluffy silvery seed-heads.

This simple little design features a few flowers from my 'Tetra-rose' with its own bronze leaves. The chosen container is glazed greeny-bronze and even the driftwood has a hint of that colour. The *montana* flowers seem to last quite well in water but the hybrids are a bit more temperamental. If you submerge them for an hour after defoliating it sometimes makes a difference but I cannot guarantee it!

The camellia is a flower that has everything as far as the flower arranger is concerned—wonderful colouring, flawless texture and exquisite shape. I love using them in my arrangements although I can hardly bear to cut them on long stems and rob the bush of so much beauty at one stroke. Instead, I make do with just two or three flowers on short stems. This does not necessarily mean small arrangements. It is amazing what can be done with a bit of ingenuity. I find the best way is to make an outline of some suitable material and then use these lovely flowers for highlights.

In this design I have made use of four pieces of wisteria which I have had for many years. They were bleached white when I bought them but for this design something more bold and dramatic was needed. After some thought and, I must admit, some soul-searching, I decided to paint them matt black. Once this had been done it was irreversible so I hope I shan't live to regret it!

The tall, waisted, black container has two separate sections for holding water which seemed just right for the idea which had been forming in my mind. After much trial and error, taking a considerable amount of time, I was able to interlock three of the pieces into an interesting shape for the upper part of the container. The vertical curlicue was the first to be impaled on to the pin-holder. Then the two other pieces were slotted into each other and hooked around the first piece and fitted into the same section. The lower swirling piece was then impaled on to the pin-holder in the lower section. The outline was now complete and all that was needed were the highlights. Two of the short-stemmed red camellias were added at the top and two lower down to complete the picture. Even after the flowers have fallen the foliage will stay fresh for a long time and other flowers such as carnations could be added in their place. Alternatively, the leaves could be preserved for other arrangements by the use of glycerine. They will take about four weeks to reach the polished brown leather state.

Camellias are not hard to grow provided they are planted in lime-free soil and they appear to be much hardier than one is generally led to believe. They are best grown in a westerly or sheltered northerly aspect against a wall or in dappled woodland where they will receive protection from the frost. Frost is the one big problem. If the flowers become frosted and cannot thaw out before the sun shines on them their petals will be completely ruined with unsightly brown marks. Even though I grow mine in the greenhouse every year when they are due to flower I cover the greenhouse glass with shading to prevent this happening. I have been doing this now for the past six years and have had no trouble.

One of my favourite flowers of late Spring is the *Polygonatum × hybridum* better known as 'Soloman's seal'. Its arching stems with pendulous clusters of tubular flowers of white tipped with green are a welcome sight in the shady border at this time of the year. Even when the flowers die they have not outlived their usefulness. Because of their dramatic form they still make wonderful outlines for modern designs and the long curved stems also make them ideal for use in pedestal arrangements in the grand manner.

I have noticed that non-flower arrangers do not cherish this plant as we do. It is usually left to fend for itself in some neglected part of the garden. Little do they know that with some tender loving care those miserable specimens will grow into impressive plants up to four feet high.

This tall, pale, greeny-bronze container seems to show off this type of flower to perfection. A copy of a Japanese-type pot, it certainly caused me some problems in the making but not in its use. For this arrangement I have impaled on to the pin-holder three of these lovely arching stems, each at a different height and angle. To add interest at the base I have made a rosette of *Hosta undulata* leaves which are beautifully marked and as lovely as any flower.

No self-respecting flower arranger should be without these plants and you should find at least a dozen to choose from in any well-stocked nursery. Of all the *hostas* my own particular favourite is the *H. Fortunei 'albo-picta'*, undoubtedly the most spectacular. At first its bright butter-yellow leaves are edged with green; later the yellow fades to primrose and the green darkens and by the time it is in flower the leaves are completely green. *H. crispula* is always the first one out in my garden each year. Its long pointed dark green leaves with prominent white margins make it a very handsome sight. I have a large clump of *H. sieboldiana* 'Elegans'. Its blue-grey, crinkled and deeply veined leaves, 8–10 inches broad, are borne on stout stalks of 10–12 inches. As you can imagine it takes up rather a lot of space but if you like doing large arrangements this is the one for you. *H. elata*, another species I grow, has leaves of more usable proportions. To get these leaves before their normal time it is well worthwhile covering your plants early in the year with cloches or, alternatively, you can pot off a small clump and take it into the greenhouse.

Lest you think the leaves only are the main attraction of this plant I must hasten to add that they all produce very delightful flowers. The tall stems of nodding trumpet-like flowers can vary from white to lilac-purple in colour depending on the species.

It is a great pity these plants are so high on the list of tasty snacks for the slug and snail population of the garden; without the necessary preventive measures the leaves can end up looking like paper doyleys.

SUMMER

SUMMER, I always feel, is really here when those aristocrats of the garden, the lilies, are in bloom. Because they look so splendid many people have the mistaken idea that they must be hard to grow. This is not the case at all but, like most of us, they have their likes and dislikes. For success with lilies you must have good drainage in the garden as they hate waterlogged soils. You can always improve the drainage by adding coarse sand or pebbles. On the other hand with light, sandy soil you should add plenty of leaf mould, peat or garden compost.

Care should be taken when selecting which varieties to grow as some are lime-tolerant, like *Lilium martagon*, and others are lime-haters, like *L. auratum*. Care should also be taken with their depth of planting which is usually given as 4–5 inches of soil above the top of the bulb. Stem-rooting lilies, such as the *auratum* and *speciosum*, can safely be planted below 6 inches of soil. However, the *candidum* and *testaceum* must be planted near the surface where in summer the sun can bake the top of the bulb. All things considered these are few rules to obey for the pleasure their sight and smell will give you year after year in the garden.

The exquisite colouring of the particular lily in this arrangement has to be seen to be believed. It is *L.* 'Journey's End', an exotic hybrid from New Zealand. The slightly reflexed petals banded with white are deep red and copiously spotted with maroon. Added to all this it has a deliciously fragrant perfume. Last year, when I grew it in the greenhouse, it was of mammoth proportions but now it has been moved out into the garden where it is subject to the vagaries of the weather it is smaller and accordingly much more useful for flower arrangements. The modern bronze-green container of mine which I chose for this design was made from three sections. The front piece is wider at the bottom than the top and the back piece is a similar shape but has been reversed. Finally, in the centre and near the top of these two sections, a 2-inch deep round pot to hold water has been attached. Thus my pot has two different appearances depending on which way round it is used. Two pots, in fact, for the price of one!

Three separate pieces of silvery-grey driftwood are used for the outline of the arrangement. The vertical piece, re-emphasizing the line of the lily petals, is impaled on the pin-holder whilst the other two pieces have been hooked on to the container. With such a splendid flower to show off any other additions would be superfluous.

It always astounds me that some gardeners look upon the orangey-yellow Peruvian lily (*Alstroemeria aurantiaca*) as an invasive weed. But I am happy to see it still grows in many cottage gardens and old herbaceous borders. I have a large clump in my garden and its solid block of bright colour brightens up the border even on the dullest of days. This species is a native of Chile so I wonder why it is known as the Peruvian lily? On second thoughts, perhaps I can understand—Chile lily would be a misnomer for one with such a fiery colour! Another interesting thing about this plant is the way its leaves twist. If you look at them closely you will see the leaves are actually produced upside down and the twist turns the leaf over bringing the underside uppermost.

If you have a sunny, sheltered spot in the garden with good drainage it is well worthwhile growing some of its more sophisticated sisters, the beautiful *Ligtu* hybrids in varied colours of cream, apricot, orange and shades of pink. As the roots are extremely brittle always buy pot-grown plants and take great care when planting not to damage the roots. You can, of course, grow them from seed if you can bear to wait a couple of years for the flowers. Sow them in February/March where you intend them to flower and then you will have no transplanting problems. In all but the mildest districts, however, the plants will need some protection such as a layer of peat, bracken or straw during the winter months.

In this design a black painted piece of wood has been placed vertically with a smaller piece added on the right-hand side at the base to give it some extra visual weight. The two *Alstroemeria* flower heads have then been added to the left in order to achieve a pleasing balance and good colour impact.

Although I have used paint in this instance there are many other ways of colouring driftwood. Coloured shoe polish, for example, can be quite effective for giving wood a subtle shade. If, however, you want to darken wood try using a stain. Wood stains can easily be obtained to simulate various finishes but do experiment on a piece of similar wood to make quite sure the colour is exactly what you require. If it is not right your precious driftwood may be ruined for ever.

Staining does not produce a shine. If it is required this can easily be given by rubbing with wax polish afterwards. If, however, you want to lighten the colour of your wood simply soak it in a mixture of bleach and water (half a bottle of bleach to a bucket of water) and leave overnight, then rinse and dry. You can repeat the process many times until you get the finish you desire. Be warned, great care should be taken to keep bleach well out of the reach of children and animals as accidents can so easily happen.

Having the right components is so important for modern designs. The container, the outline and the item chosen to give you the focal point or highlight are all critical. The transitional type materials used in other designs to soften the overall appearance are largely dispensed with as the main aim is to get the maximum impact with a minimum of material. In many of these designs you will notice that only outline material and just one or two flowers, with or without leaves, have been used.

The inspiration for your arrangement may be triggered off by any of the three components—a beautiful or unusual flower, some interesting outline material or an out-of-the-ordinary container. Making many of my containers, as I do, I can find no greater spur than a newly fired one. It can either be its shape, texture or colour which catches the imagination—but the more complex the container the harder it will be to select suitable materials for it. And herein lies its constant and absorbing challenge. As there is no set pattern to follow, as in the more traditional styles, your own creativity can be given full reign and new and original ideas can be explored.

However, in this instance it wasn't the container which was the source of inspiration but the flowers. The plant from which they grew was purchased at a local horticultural society's sales table and was labelled *Euphorbia* and although I was a little doubtful about its pedigree I bought it just the same as it looked so healthy. Imagine my surprise and delight when it turned out to be a *Nerium oleander* and a few clusters of its creamy-pink flowers are featured in this design. As it is a tender species I treat it like a favourite old aunt, sitting it out on the patio in all finery on warm sunny days and whisking it under cover at the first sign of inclement weather. I have already potted it on three times and its fourth re-potting is imminent for it continues to grow and grow as though not realizing that it is now located in a garden in Cheshire and not on the Mediterranean where its normal height is some 15 feet.

The subtle colour of the flowers reminded me of bamboo and this container is just a section cut from a large pole. To make sure it is waterproof I have swished polythene varnish round the inside. The outline material is dried *Edgeworthia* 'Mitsumata' which is imported from Japan. It is rather brittle, probably due to the fact that it has been bleached, and although it is a little pricey, with care it will last indefinitely. I have had mine for about 15 years and find its linear outline extremely useful and versatile. It can often be purchased from flower club sales tables but failing this try any *Ikebana* (Japanese flower arrangement) exhibition which is where mine was purchased.

Black and white photograph, page 41

I must admit to a certain fascination with designing outlines of cane and rattan. There are endless possibilities for its use with modern arrangements. The cane which I have used in this design is much easier to tame than rattan which has a tendency to fall about in all directions but the right one. This is the type of cane used for making the uprights when weaving a basket. The three pieces were soaked in water and when they were pliable tied into their predestined shapes. Always remember to make the shapes tighter than you require as they will always splay out a little when they are dried and untied. Even with just these three pieces there are endless ways in which they can be used.

Here, I have enclosed space to make it a part of the design. The black vertical triangular container has been filled with sand so that the pin-holder sits on it firmly just below the rim. Starting with the small circle and working outwards the outline slowly took shape. The loose ends of the cane were secured at their required places on the edge of the circles with minute pieces of Plasticine. For impact material I chose two 'Super Star' roses. It is a favourite rose of mine as its glowing vermilion colour makes it a real eye-catcher. It does, however, seem to have lost some of its popularity these days because of its tendency to fall prey to mildew. Recently at a show I saw another rose equally striking in its brilliant vermilion colour which I was assured by the grower is less prone in this respect. It is called 'Alexander'.

Roses must still be about the best value for money in garden plants. Each year brings its new varieties but 'Peace', 'Mischief' and 'Fragrant Cloud' take some beating in my estimation: 'Peace' for its colour, 'Mischief' for its shape, and 'Fragrant Cloud' for its delightful perfume. I was interested to read recently that my opinion of 'Fragrant Cloud' was fully endorsed at a Lincolnshire rose show where there was a class for 'One fragrant rose—to be judged by two blind persons'. There was a large entry. The blind judges gave first, second and third prizes to the only three 'Fragrant Cloud' roses entered.

Apart from its beauty and fragrance a rose can be put to many uses from making cosmetics to flavouring syllabub. I sometimes make chocolate leaves by using their green leaves as a mould but until I read about it recently I had never thought of crystallizing their petals. As there seems to be a resurgence in the use of herbs for cookery will the next in-thing be the use of flower petals and leaves as well? It might well be. Marigold petals used to be indispensable for flavouring soups and mutton dishes whilst, believe it or not, mediaeval knights feasted regularly on rose and primrose stew. But lest you think I am writing a cookery book I had better get back to flower arrangement.

Spring
The curving piece of *Sambucus racemosa* 'Plumosa Aurea' makes a pleasing outline for this grouping of *Narcissus* 'Cheerfulness'

Spring
A spray of camellias highlights this dramatic outline made from cut and fashioned dried angelica stalks

Summer
Dried sea-wrack makes the contorted outline featuring the lovely yellow *Lilium* 'Limelight'

Summer
The beaten copper container and base along with the fasciated forsythia harmonize well with the orange *Lilium* 'Enchantment'

Autumn
Thick ivy stripped from a tree makes an excellent outline for this design of yellow spider chrysanthemums and variegated ivy

Autumn
'Bonfire Night' — a modern interpretative design

Winter
Two orange paper poppies highlight this design of dried materials

Winter

The two bronze chrysanthemums and variegated camellia foliage are encompassed in the swirling outline
fashioned from bleached broom

As I mentioned earlier, rattan is not the easiest medium to tame when making outlines for modern designs. Over the years I have experimented to find the simplest way to get the most effective use from this strong-willed material with a mind of its own. There are many thicknesses which you will find suitable, from very thin to finger-thick. In the case of the very fine rattan which comes in coils I tend to use it as it is, simply looping the coils through my design, hooking them on to convenient hanging points. The material has a bleached appearance but it can easily be painted or even dyed. As you would imagine the coils are very hard to paint or even spray and I find it much easier to colour them with dye. Simply submerge the coils in a mixture of dye and leave until they are slightly darker than the shade you require and you will find that when they dry out the colour will be just right.

The thicker rattan I find easier to use when made up into individual shapes which can then be used by interlocking them to make fascinating patterns. The rattan is soaked as usual and while damp and pliable cut into long lengths, manipulated into interesting shapes and tied where necessary. I usually make three of each type although I do not use them all at once. The best way I have found to deal with the finger-thick rattan is to make it into loops of varying sizes so enabling enclosed space to be part of one's designs. Both these thicknesses can be painted or sprayed more easily than the thin coiled variety.

In this design I have made use of three similar-type shapes and whether I could ever get them into the same outline again is another matter. They remind me of those metal puzzles we had when I was a child which kept me quiet for hours—and come to think of it, so did these pieces of rattan!

In this dark brown container a core of floral foam was placed in the top part of the left-hand 'funnel' and the top vertical piece of rattan was pushed firmly into it. The second piece was then reversed and threaded through the tight coils at the top of the first piece. Finally, as you can see, the lower piece was reversed and threaded through the loop of the second piece. The right-hand 'funnel' was left empty and used for topping up the water without disturbing the design. Two flowers from the *Hemerocallis* (otherwise known as the day lily because of its fleeting life) completed the picture. As long as the outline is safely anchored it is a simple matter to renew the flowers as they die off.

Not only has the day lily a beautiful flower, it also has very attractive foliage. It is probably one of the first to appear in the garden each year and its lovely fresh green shoots are a delight to use in spring arrangements. They grow equally well in sun or partial shade and spread quite quickly—an attribute which is always an advantage to flower arrangers.

The origin of these beautifully polished tan stems may puzzle you if you have not come across them before. They are from the *Macleaya cordata* (still known to many flower arrangers as *Bocconia*). It is a useful herbaceous perennial but take care when siting it as it grows to a height of 7–8 feet. As they spread by means of underground suckers they can be invasive plants. Mine regularly appear in various parts of the border and I was rather indignant when finer specimens than my own suddenly appeared in the garden next door having tunnelled under an old stone wall to reach their new home. They produce plumes of tiny coral flowers in July and August and if you pick them in bud they are far more attractive. A note of caution, however—the cut stems and leaves exude a strong yellow dye, so keep them well away from your clothes.

When I tidy up the garden each year the few unused stems which dry beautifully like this are cut and kept for outline material or to make very superior false stems. Being tall these plants do get blown about in the wind but I resist staking them and am always rewarded with some lovely curved stems. Here I have used one such stem along with a straighter piece to give extra height and balance to the design. And because of the tan colour of the stalks a favourite polished terra-cotta container of mine seemed to be just right for it. The pin-holder has been hidden behind some tan and cream flints which were picked up on the beach at Sheringham in Norfolk. Some of my best flower arranging treasures have been gleaned whilst on holiday in various parts of the country. They are happy reminders of such holidays, far nicer than anything bought from 'Ye Olde Gifte Shoppe'.

The splendid rose which inspired this design is as near perfect a rose as I have ever grown so I simply had to show it off. However, I must admit it was grown in the greenhouse and not out of doors. By this means I have roses much earlier than I would do normally and at the same time they are in first-class condition. After some research and a great deal of thought I eventually planted three of the hybrid tea, 'Fragrant Cloud'. It has large and shapely flowers of vivid vermilion-scarlet borne on strong stems and, as a bonus, a delightful fragrance.

Garden roses last well in arrangements provided they are cut in bud and given a long drink. Florists' roses, however, sometimes present problems and it is a good idea to give them the 'boiling water treatment'. Submerge the bottom inch of the stem in boiling water for 30 seconds making sure that the leaves and flower are not damaged by the steam by wrapping them loosely in a cloth or polythene bag. They should then have a long drink in deep water before being arranged when, hopefully, they will behave themselves.

With its infinite variety of shape, texture and colour—no two pieces are ever alike—driftwood has for me a special fascination. It seems to enhance all flower arrangements, traditional, naturalistic or modern. When you have only a few flowers to use it can make an otherwise insignificant design into something large and dramatic.

Over the years I have acquired quite a large collection, varying from small pieces useful for hiding pin-holders to large, imposing pieces 4–5 feet tall which are works of art in their own right. Driftwood (to quote the NAFAS schedule definitions) is 'any type of dried wood, roots or bark'. It can come from the sea, from rivers or the countryside. Some of my most sculptural pieces have been found on the beach, having been tossed around in the sea for a great length of time before being washed ashore. This gave them softly rounded features and a bleached appearance.

The wood found in rivers or by the banks has been brought down by flood water. More often than not it is broken tree roots or branches and is usually angular. Driftwood from the countryside, found in woods and hedges, is much chunkier. It consists of partially rotted tree stumps and branches. Often they are partially hidden in the undergrowth and, like an ice-berg, you see only the tip. An eye for such hidden treasures develops and like a dog trained to sniff out truffles I have become an expert in the art. Some pieces at first seem of little interest but a gentle probing with a stick, teasing out the mass of woodland detritus, may reveal a masterpiece. Half the fun is in the hunting.

Driftwood found on the beach or in rivers usually needs little or no preparation. This has been done naturally by the water. Anything found in woodland or the countryside always needs some attention. I usually clean it roughly on the spot to get rid of any attendant wild life. When I get home I give it a thorough going-over with a wire brush to loosen any rotted bits and pieces. I then hose it at high pressure, let it dry out naturally and, if necessary, treat it with Rentokil. Only after this treatment do I bring it into the house to consider its possibilities.

Don't be in too much of a hurry to trim and alter the shape of your wood. Consider it well from all angles; once you have sawn it you can't start again.

In this design I have built up a sculptured outline with four pieces of similarly grained and coloured driftwood. The three stems of *Lilium regale* have been inserted in a tall brown container which has two placements for flowers and is hidden away at the back.

I do not go along with those people who remove the ripe anthers from the stamens of the lily to prevent the falling pollen marking the petals. I prefer them as nature intended; they seem to lose some of their magic when this is done.

When I was given a small innocent-looking plant of the yellow daisy-like *Inula helenium*, a variety sometimes known as 'Elecampane', little did I think it would turn out to be such a giant. In three years it has grown into a very large clump and is still increasing every year. It is a back-of-the-border plant as it grows to a height of 6–8 feet with the lower leaves reaching the size of dinner plates. Its flowers, with their thread-like petals, are carried on branched stems in August. I see from my gardening encyclopaedia that there are other sizes of this plant suitable for the rock garden so it would appear that as well as my giant there are also some dwarfs!

The *I. helenium* has been used since Roman times for culinary and medicinal purposes. The Romans used it as a vegetable and as a conserve and in the nineteenth century it became very popular as a medicine for chest complaints. Farriers also used it as a medicine for horses.

In this design with driftwood three flowers from this plant form the highlight backed with leaves from the *Mahonia aquifolium*, a very useful ground cover plant and a very tolerant one, too. However, the *M. bealei* is the flower arranger's first choice of this species. It not only has splendid foliage but in those comparatively flowerless winter months from December to February produces its lemon-yellow sweet scented racemes of flowers for our delight.

The foliage of this plant also glycerines beautifully. This is a very simple process which preserves various plant materials indefinitely. Simply pour into a jar one measure of glycerine to two measures of hot water and stir well. Although the initial cost of glycerine is quite expensive the mixture can be used over and over again making it a well worthwhile exercise. Try and pick unblemished foliage when it is at its peak of perfection. Scrape and split the bottom inch or so and stand in at least two inches of the mixture. It will take 4–6 weeks to preserve *Mahonia* and when it is ready it will have taken on a polished dark brown finish. If you prefer a lighter colour stand the leaves in the sun for a couple of weeks after preservation.

Beech is probably the most common foliage to be glycerined but this is only one of many foliages that can be preserved in this way. Some worth trying are *Camellia*, *Choisya ternata*, *Eucalyptus*, *Grevillea robusta*, *Pittosporum tenuifolium* and *Sorbus aria* (whitebeam). Before preserving larger leaves such as the *Aspidistra* and *Fatsia japonica* mop the leaves well on both sides with the glycerined mixture and then stand the stems in it. This will prevent the leaves drying out at the tips before the mixture has reached them.

There would appear to be little affinity between plumbing and flower arranging but a study of this design may lead you to think that there is. It also shows that even the most unlikely materials are all grist to the mill as far as the flower arranger is concerned. Seeing some discarded short lengths of ¼-inch diameter copper tubing after a repair job had been done at home I boldly asked if I could keep them. Trying to explain to a mystified plumber about flower arranging in general and outlines in particular is not an easy matter. Nevertheless, although he did not seem very convinced about my motives he let me have them with a nod and shake of the head.

Copper tubing is not an easy medium to handle but with patience I gradually coaxed it into an interesting outline suitable for a modern design. The next problem was to find a means of standing it upright as it was quite heavy. After trial and error this was finally resolved by inserting a short piece of wood dowelling into each end of the tubing so making it possible to impale them on to the pin-holder at the desired angle. No doubt this will have to be renewed periodically when it splinters and ceases to hold firm.

When creating any kind of design never be satisfied until your mechanics are foolproof. It is so frustrating to have the whole thing fall apart when you are putting in your last placement all because of lack of attention to such vital details.

After applying much elbow grease to the copper tubing to obtain a high polish I cast about for a container which would enhance this rather unusual outline. Once again I could not resist using a favourite terra-cotta container made whilst I was attending pottery classes at the art school. I suppose everyone has a container which just seems right for most arrangements and for me this is the one.

Enclosed space figures prominently in modern arrangements and it is as much a part of the design as the flowers themselves. Glowing copper and terra-cotta made me think of the 'Enchantment' lilies I had growing in the garden so to complete the design one was positioned in the upper space and one in the lower. Orangey-brown pieces of flint suitably placed hid the pin-holder from view.

For reliability it is hard to improve on 'Enchantment' lilies which I have grown over many trouble-free years. 'Cinnabar', a glowing maroon-red, and 'Paprika', a rich deep crimson, are both worthy companions for it. All three are descended from *Lilium tigrinum* and have inherited the strong constitution of this plant.

'Be Prepared' is not just a motto for the Scouts; it applies to flower arrangers, too. You need never be without an arrangement if you follow this suggestion. I call it 'outline planning'. Select two or three containers and in each one arrange some suitable outline. It can be of wood, metal or dried plant material; it really does not matter as long as it is something which will last indefinitely. Each design should be quite different, the only similarity being that all that is needed to complete the picture is the addition of a few fresh flowers. When you have these stand-bys ready for immediate embellishment many a last-minute panic will be avoided.

Here is an example of the type of thing I mean. The chosen container is shiny black, oblong, and incised with a pattern. The two pieces of driftwood I have used had become rather blemished with water marks so once again out came my pot of blackboard paint and they were given a new lease of life. The vertical piece of wood which comes to a fine point has been slotted into a thick, dried piece of teasel stem to make it easier to impale on a pin-holder. The other delightfully twisted piece is most accommodating and simply sits on the container without the need for any hidden aids.

The pink 'Garnet' roses which provide the necessary impact are actually a single floriferous stem with no less than nine flowers. Normally, these dainty roses are regarded as florists' flowers and are much used at weddings and christenings. These are from my own greenhouse where a number of cuttings poked into the soil five years ago have provided me with an abundance of flowers ever since.

The teasel, incidentally, is a very useful plant in many ways in that it can be used effectively in its plain green state, or when its myriad flowers come out and turn it mauve, or when it has dried off, either on the plant or after cutting. And, as I have mentioned, its hollow stem can provide a sturdy support for less robust material. But be careful—when you cut the dried stems use a small saw and not secateurs or scissors which will split them. Finally, if you still have any left at the end of the season you can whiten and glitter them for your Christmas decorations.

All my teasels—and those of many of my friends—originally came from a few seeds which I collected from a dried stem found growing on top of a ruined wall of Whalley Abbey in Lancashire. These plants are biennials but once you have them, and as long as you don't use the hoe too much, you will always have them. In the winter they look dazzling after a hoar frost, just like great Christmas tree decorations. And word of their existence quickly spread round the local goldfinch population and these delightful birds visit the garden regularly to extract the seeds and scatter some for me at the same time.

Chincherinchee, the flower used in this design, trips off the tongue readily enough which is more than can be said of its botanical name, *Ornithogalum thyrsoides*!

It does not seem all that many years ago since this plant was discovered by the florists amid a blaze of publicity. Its initial popularity seems to have waned somewhat but it is still used by flower arrangers though more as a filler for mass arrangements rather than on its own. Nevertheless, its dainty star-like flowers have a certain appeal.

Chincherinchees were initially imported from South Africa but today they mostly come from Guernsey and occasionally from Holland and can be found at the florists' from July until October. Although they are not hardy in this country they can be grown in a cool greenhouse or frame for early flowering. If, however, you wish to grow them in open ground plant the bulbs 3–4 inches deep from mid-April onwards when they will give you a fine display. They should be lifted in autumn before the frosts come, and stored indoors.

The main attribute of these flowers is their long-lasting quality and they will last at least a month in an arrangement. As the bottom flowers die they can be easily nipped off to keep your arrangement looking pristine fresh until the buds have all opened and you have had your money's worth.

It was not just the heavenly affinity which made me choose a moon container for these star-like flowers. Chincherinchees can appear rather stalky in an arrangement and to overcome this problem I have placed them so that they overlap. Glossy-leaved, dark green ivy is a marvellous foil for white flowers and a whorl of leaves has been placed to the left of centre to create good balance. And to give more impact and visual appeal the moon stands on a black scroll base.

In the Spring section of this book I used a similar type of moon container giving details of its construction. In this instance, instead of covering it with anaglypta paper I used sheet pewter. This can be obtained from the larger handicraft shops along with sheet copper but the latter is much harder to work than pewter. It is vitally important that the pewter—which I hammered for an interesting textural effect—should be cut exactly to size as the seams are butt-jointed. Leave for a couple of days to make sure the pewter has well and truly adhered then wipe it over with patina (also obtainable from the craft shops). When it is dry buff up with a soft duster so that the highlights reappear on the raised surfaces. This, like the previous moon, is not waterproof and a small narrow container for water can easily be placed in the opening. With dried arrangements just arrange in a piece of floral foam which has been wedged in place.

When we moved into our present home some 15 years ago the stone walls surrounding the garden were bare but today they are all covered with a cascading mass of nine different species of that indispensable evergreen climber, the ivy. If you grow it in the garden you need never be without attractive foliage to go with those flowers you have unexpectedly been given, even in the dreariest winter months. Of course, there are those who cannot stand the sight of it and tear it down, even in the countryside where often it is clothing just a dead tree or something which would otherwise be unsightly.

The common green ivy was the first to be grown and I still find it very useful in spite of its more sophisticated sisters I now cultivate. Its dark green shining leaves are a wonderful foil for most flowers. My *Hedera canariensis* 'Variegata' started life as a pot plant which just grew and grew. When it got quite out of hand and was taking over the hall I moved it outside to cover an unused clothes-post. It is now like a huge shrub and is frequently used as a cosy roosting place by the local bird population. The other ivies have all been grown from cuttings from various people over the years and they tend to be known by the donor's name rather than that found in any gardening book— a habit which tends to flummox some of my more knowledgeable friends.

So that you will know which I am talking about I must use their proper names. They are *H. helix* 'Buttercup', 'Goldheart', 'Silver Queen' and 'Digitata'; *H. colchica* and *H. c. dentata* 'Variegata', and a very delightful small-leaved green variety with frilly parsley-like edges. So far I have been unable to identify it.

As I have already indicated, ivies are very easy to grow. They will thrive in any soil and almost any situation. The variegated forms, however, colour best in south- or west-facing positions. Even though I am constantly cutting mine for my own and my friends' arrangements, they still have to be pruned regularly to keep them within bounds. You can grow them easily from 3–5-inch cuttings taken from the tips of shoots in July and August or alternatively from ripe shoots in October and November when the soft tips should be removed.

On this occasion, with my two pieces of beautiful 'Buttercup' yellow ivy I chose three brilliant 'Super Star' roses for their intensity of colour. The shiny black dual-compartment container and the black wood seemed to make the flowers and foliage glow more than ever. As you can see, the blackened branch has been reversed and a short convenient twig enabled me to impale it on the pin-holder. In modern designs this is a good ploy to use as the wood usually looks more dramatic this way and less naturalistic.

Two fascinating plants which I used to grow in the greenhouse have now been banished to the garden because of their rampant growth. Anyone who has grown either the *Passiflora caerulea* (passion flower) or *Cobea scandens* (cup and saucer plant) will know what I mean.

Five years ago I took the plunge and planted my passion flower out of doors in a sheltered sunny spot on trellis-work against a wall. Despite a particularly hard winter and frequent frosts it is still flourishing although much of the top growth has to be cut back each year. Over the years, in fact, I have found that a lot of plants are much hardier than might be imagined.

For those who might not know, the passion flower's name derives from the fact that the parts of the flower and foliage are all symbolic of Christ's crucifixion. The crown of thorns is represented by the rays of the corona, the nails by the three stigmas, the wounds by the five stamens while the ten petals represent the apostles. The palmate leaves depict the hands of Christ's persecutors and the tendrils the whips with which they scourged him.

The flowers are about three inches across and make a wonderful sight throughout the summer months. Once they start flowering they continue in great profusion until the frosts come. In hot summers they also produce an abundance of golden egg-shaped fruits. I am told that the seeds and jelly-like substance surrounding them are delicious to eat, the flavour resembling that of mulberries.

The passion flower can be propagated by seed or by cuttings which is the way I prefer. Take 3–4-inch-long stem sections in July/August and insert them in the usual sand and peat potting medium. If you do not possess a propagating frame they will do equally well in a pot placed in a plastic bag on the window sill. Put some sort of scaffolding of twigs or sticks inside the bag to keep the plastic from touching the cuttings and thereby preventing damping-off. When they have rooted, pot off singly into three-inch containers and as they grow move them into larger pots. And eventually—unless you keep them under control by judicious pruning—you will, as I was, be driven to moving them out of doors.

You may wonder why I use these flowers for an arrangement when their beauty is so transitory, lasting as they do for only a day. It is because I think it well worthwhile, even for such a short time, to be able to study the flower's special beauty more closely and wonder at it.

It only takes a matter of minutes to put such a design together. I chose a palish, greeny-brown container made from two cylinders, one taller than the other and joined together with a foot added to each. Small pieces of floral foam were fitted into the two sections and just two trails of the plant were caught round the pieces of dried vine which provided support for the design.

Growing plants from seeds I have saved and cuttings I have taken or, as in this case, from tiny bulbils, always gives me a great thrill. It is a challenge I cannot resist. Take the lovely *Lilium tigrinum* (tiger lily), for example. In the garden I now have at least two dozen or more that originally came from just three or four bulbils. These are the small immature bulbs which form at the leaf axils of certain species of lilies. And it is not a case of green fingers; it is a case of 'TLC' (tender loving care). That is what is needed to make them grow. There is no mystique and anyone can do it.

The bulbils were planted in the garden in prepared soil in a sunny position. I carefully marked them, of course, so they would not be hoed down by accident. The first year they each produced two three-inch-long leaves and the following year a short stem of leaves about five inches in height. The third year I had the pleasure of seeing just one flower on each. Since then they have flourished and are now about 4–5 feet tall. They usually carry about 6–8 flowers each and this year one carried 13 which was a marvellous sight.

They are bright orange-red spotted with purple-black and have prominent anthers with dark red pollen. This can be rather a menace as it stains everything it comes into contact with but in spite of this I never remove the anthers.

Deciding on the right container for a certain arrangement needs quite a lot of thought. Its shape, colour and texture all play a part and whether it is to match or to contrast is another question to be considered. After some deliberation I decided on this dark reddish-brown container, the colour of the lily's anthers. And although it is slightly smaller than I would have wished for the size of the arrangement, the addition of the two bamboo mats makes it acceptable.

The brown curved piece of wood is from a vine growing on the side of the house which is grown more for its stems and leaves than its grapes! The piece was persuaded into a lovely curved loop whilst it was still green and when it matured it provided me with a ready-made outline.

The rather unusual container was inspired, like many of my pots, by the Japanese. It was made from eight separate parts which were joined together before firing. All except the flat top piece were thrown on the wheel. The bowl was joined to the ring underneath while the five assorted funnels were inserted into the flat piece of clay which in its turn was joined on to the bowl. From all the work involved the non-potter will begin to realize just why some of the more unusual pots appear to be rather expensive to buy.

I make a rod for my own back, I know, by being the sort of person who can't throw flowers away until they are completely dead. Arrangements have to be pulled apart before disposing of them if there is a sign of life in any one flower. And it is often the gladioli tops which outlast the rest of the arrangement. Hence this design made from the last-gasp florets of a delightful white one rescued from such an arrangement.

I have always been keen on green and white arrangements especially on hot sunny days when they look so cool and crisp. So from the garden I gathered a few trails of *Vinca major* 'Elegantissima' (the variegated periwinkle), a curved piece of *Hedera canariensis* 'Variegata' and a few handsome leaves from the *Hosta crispula*. It is always important to condition your materials and it is doubly so with foliage when it is to be the main part of your design.

The easiest way to treat foliage is to immerse it in water overnight and I find my rain-water tank in the garden is excellent for this purpose. If you do not have such a convenient tank a large bowl or sink or even the bath can be used instead. This treatment not only makes the foliage last longer but cleans it at the same time. If, however, it is particularly dirty like the long-lasting evergreens sometimes are, they can be swished through warm water containing some washing-up liquid before immersing in cold water. But, of course, there are always exceptions to the rule. Do not immerse any *grey* leaves or their lovely velvety surfaces will become waterlogged and spoilt. I always give these the 'boiling water' treatment, making sure that while they have their toes in the boiling water for 30 seconds their heads are covered with a loose cloth or piece of plastic. I then place them in shallow water in a dark place overnight. If you take the trouble to condition your materials like this next day you will find the turgid leaves and foliage at their peak for arranging.

In this design I have placed the curved piece of ivy in the top section of the pale green container with three *hosta* leaves following the same line. The long trails of periwinkle have then been placed to give an opposing curve starting in the top and finishing in the bottom section. Finally, my white gladioli has been added to highlight the arrangement.

The design for this container was taken from a popular type of *Ikebana* pot which is sometimes made of bamboo. The top section is only two inches deep and so is the opening at the bottom. Both these sections easily accommodate a pin-holder which makes it an ideal container for modern arrangements where concealment of the mechanics with little plant material is essential but not always easy to accomplish.

Give a man or woman a piece of land to turn into a garden and the chances are that one of the first things planted will be a rose tree. It is our national flower, painters paint it, poets and song-writers wax lyrical over it and flower arrangers would be lost without it.

We normally think only of the hybrid tea and floribunda when roses are mentioned but there is so much more to this splendid species as any garden book will tell you. Mind you, the roses we flower arrangers like are not always the ones the experts admire. In interpretative work we tend to go for the subtle shades like 'Royal Highness' with its pale cream-pink perfectly shaped blooms, or 'Blue Moon' with its soft lilac flowers and a new one called 'Julia's Rose' with its petals a subtle blend of parchment and copper tones. However, in modern designs where immediate impact is needed bright and bold is usually the order of the day. Some of my own favourites are 'Cheshire Life' with its brilliant vermilion-orange blooms; 'Whisky Mac' which provides me with golden tangerine flowers; 'Fragrant Cloud', a delightful coral-red with a fragrant perfume, and 'Mischief', a rich pink with a perfect form. And who can talk of roses without mentioning 'Peace', the most universally favoured variety ever introduced.

When cutting roses for your arrangements it is worthwhile taking a little extra trouble to make sure they stay fresh as long as possible. Cut them at the coolest part of the day, either morning or evening, choosing partly opened buds. Remove the thorns and any surplus foliage and, if possible, stand them up to their necks in water in a cool, dark place for up to twelve hours. Do not be tempted to arrange them immediately or you will be disappointed as they will invariably wilt. Florists' roses can be a bit more temperamental and even when given a long drink they still sometimes droop. If they are taken out of the arrangement and re-cut and floated on tepid water for several hours they will usually revive. Some arrangers swear by the 'burn-the-ends-in-a-flame' method whilst others stand the stem ends in two inches of boiling water, taking care, of course, to protect the blooms from the steam. Whilst I use these methods with other types of flowers I have never found it necessary with roses.

The container I have used for this arrangement came about by accident rather than design. It should have been a cylindrical container on the left with a small container on the right joined by an open-work section. When the kiln was opened it was in three separate pieces—a not uncommon occurrence, as all potters will know. I was able to rescue the cylindrical part to which I attached the broken right section with impact adhesive. The third unusable piece was thrown away. I must say I have been quite happy with the container which evolved and even think it looks better now than it did in its original form!

Some fine bleached driftwood gives height to my arrangement and the coral 'Elizabeth of Glamis' roses complete this simple modern line design.

AUTUMN

AUTUMN officially begins in September and one of the few flowers which effects the transition between the seasons is the late-flowering *Galtonia candicans* which is sometimes referred to as the summer hyacinth. It does not seem to be very widely grown even among flower arrangers though its tall spikes of slightly scented white flowers make an attractive display when other plants in the border are past their best. The bulbs should be planted six inches deep and six inches apart any time from February to April. They prefer a well-drained sunny border and once they are planted should be left undisturbed to establish themselves and so multiply. They are also suitable for greenhouse cultivation. Plant 3–5 bulbs in a 6–8-inch pot in October for flowering in May and June.

For height in this simple modern line arrangement I have chosen two stems of *Cyperus esculentus* with its leaf-like bracts resembling umbrella ribs. This genus of moisture-loving plants has a mind-boggling 550 species. And it never ceases to amaze me that someone, somewhere, somehow managed to identify them all! The tender species—in this country at least—include *C. papyrus* from the Nile delta with which the ancient Egyptians used to make a kind of paper. It was prepared by cutting the central pith of the stems into long strips, laying others across, moistening, pressing, drying and polishing so that it was possible to write upon it·with a reed-pen.

Although I grew my first *C. esculentus* as a pot plant in the greenhouse it seems to be quite a hardy species. It is now growing strongly in various parts of the garden and has even decided to take a dip in the garden pond. One self-seeded plant in the soil of the greenhouse is now of such mammoth proportions that I shall not be able to use it unless, of course, I am called upon to do a six-feet-tall water arrangement! Normally, however, this plant grows to about two feet which is a much more useful height. So here we have it backing two smallish flowers of the *G. candicans* along with three leaves of the *Iris foetidissima*. To enhance the green and white design further I chose a Japanese-type container and hid the pin-holder behind an interesting piece of white coral.

White containers are very hard to use successfully in flower arrangements except in green and white designs such as this one. Although, theoretically, white is neutral it is such a dominant factor when it is the colour of your container—unlike black, another neutral, which seems just right for a container for any design.

I suppose most people looking at this design would mentally note that it included geraniums although, to be strictly correct, they are *Zonal pelargoniums*; from the Greek word *pelargos*—a stork. Well named, I think you will agree, as the ripe seed-head does resemble the head and beak of that particular bird.

They must be one of the most versatile flowers we have, whether they are used for bedding out, in window-boxes or as pot-plants. They can be timed to bloom at any season of the year and even trained as standards or half-standards. The newer hybrid varieties, which include the splendid double-flowered specimens, range in colour from white, pink, rose and salmon to scarlet and cerise. I believe it is easy, and of course very much cheaper, to grow them from seed; something I must definitely try.

Usually, black and white photographs of flower arrangements leave a lot to be imagined by the viewer but in this instance it is actually in full colour! The contorted piece of wood, which has seen better days and has now been condemned to matt black, has been reversed in use from the actual way it grew. This is a ploy I frequently use and it is surprising how often it looks better that way. Just three of these lovely white flowers grouped together in one of the funnels of the container complete the picture.

The two black bases were cut along with others from an old discarded garden gate. In modern designs the bases as well as the containers must be equally suitable. Velvet-covered ones with braided borders and fringes are definitely out, just as a classic urn would be as a container. A collection of wooden bases in geometric shapes are possibly the most useful to have and can easily be made even with a minimum of carpentry skills. These can simply be painted or covered with felt, suede, or any other suitable material. Perspex, plastic, metal, straw and bamboo are other media from which modern bases can be made.

Be discriminating in the way you use a base and remember that not every arrangement needs one. Unless it appears to be an integral part of your design and to take it away would ruin the overall picture, think twice before you use it. Sometimes, when a container is a little smaller than you would have wished, the addition of a base will give you the good balance you are striving for.

I know many people use bases in the home mainly to protect their furniture from scratches and watermarks. This is possibly why many exhibitors at shows have got that 'base' habit and seem incapable of doing an exhibit without one.

A trip round most flower arrangers' gardens by non-flower arrangers will invariably bring forth many a 'what's *this?*' and a 'what's *that?*' and, not infrequently, a 'what on earth have you got *there?*' for such is the unusual stuff we need to grow to complement the flowers we arrange. And high up in the last category comes a border plant called *Photolacca americana*, or poke weed. It grows from 3 to 5 feet high and is not particularly remarkable until the flowering season. From June to September it produces erect spikes, 3–4 inches long, of greenish flowers followed by fruits which are the same colour to begin with but which turn to deep purple as they ripen. And at this stage they must be handled with care. If squeezed they squirt a deep crimson juice, thus giving rise to its other name of red ink plant.

For this design a bold outline of driftwood has been assembled in a suitable container— and by 'a suitable container' I mean a large and stable one. This pot was especially made for such an occasion. It is slab-built and has a base dimension of ten by eight inches so that when it is filled with water it is as steady as a rock. Whenever I catch a glimpse of it on my container shelves it always reminds me of the base of the Eiffel Tower, so not only is it very substantial—it looks it!

Four separate pieces of wood similar in colour and texture were used in this design. No mechanical aids whatsoever were called upon for its construction. It was a case of trial and error, wedging piece after piece in various positions until I obtained a firm, and at the same time pleasing, assemblage.

Making suitable outlines with driftwood is quite a challenge for an arranger as it is not always easy to fix the wood in the required position. Over the years devices have been brought out for this very purpose. However, I made my own clamps fastened to lead bases long before they were sold in the shops and I am happy to say they are still going strong. Another useful home-made device is the screw-type base. This can easily be made by melting lead and pouring it into a suitable tin which has a long brass screw in the centre pointing upwards. To use it all one has to do is to drill a hole at the correct angle in the base of the wood which you wish to fix and screw it into place. The larger and heavier the base the larger and heavier the wood it will hold.

In this design sprays of poke weed in their greenish fruit stage complement the subtle greenish-yellow of the cactus dahlia 'Klanstad Kerkrade' and contrast with the peacock-blue glazed container.

'Go for foliage and not for flowers' is a good maxim for flower arrangers with smaller gardens. After all, you can always buy flowers but lovely and unusual foliage is much harder to come by.

Mind you, some of my favourite foliage plants are more like trees than plants and take up quite a bit of room. The *Onopordum acanthium* (Scotch thistle) whose magnificent silver leaves I have featured in this design is typical. It is a biennial and once planted will seed itself without any trouble for years to come. They grow to a height of 8–10 feet and they are a back-of-the-border plant and look equally well in a shrubbery or wild garden. They are real eye-catchers by day and by night they make a wonderful ghostly sight when seen by the light of the moon.

Not only are the leaves of this plant useful but their curved stems bearing thistle-like heads make excellent outlines. I prefer to use these heads before they show their colour as they are much more attractive at that stage of growth. As with other grey foliage do not submerge in water to condition; simply boil the ends of the stems and leave overnight for a long drink before arranging. The more mature the leaves are the better they will last.

Other grey-leaved plants of similarly large proportions are the *Cynara scolymus* (the globe artichoke) and the *C. cardunculus* (the cardoon). These are herbaceous perennials and thrive in deep rich loam in an open and sunny position. To get the best out of these plants reduce the number of shoots to two or three each spring. The offsets can then be used to make new plantings as the parent plant deteriorates considerably after three years and is not worth growing on. In this way you will ensure a constant supply of first-class flower heads.

The thistle-like flowers of these plants are far more impressive than those of the *Onopordum*. They are equally attractive in arrangements either in their unopened state, when they are showing colour, or finally as an enormous dried flower. I find it easier to let them dry on the plant until they have turned a lovely dark brown when I cut them and finish the drying process off indoors by hanging them upside down. If, however, the flowers start to disintegrate, fear not, as the central boss of pale-fawn coloured fluff is equally attractive. As with other fluffy seed-heads, spray with hair lacquer to help retain their fuzz.

To enhance further my splendid leaves on this design I chose a grey compote-type container. The tallest leaf is all of three feet in height and two smaller leaves, suitably curved, were added to complete the outline. Four enormous bright red florets from the base of a gladioli provide the highlight to this bold arrangement.

At a quick glance you might think that this was an arrangement of pineapples impaled like lollipops on sticks. But what attractive sticks! Pale green blotched with maroon, they are the stalks of the exotic *Eucomis comosa*, a plant of South African origin. Its name comes from the Greek word *eukomus* meaning 'beautiful haired' and refers to that leafy tuft surmounting the flower spike. Not unexpectedly they are more commonly known as the pineapple flower and the two heads I have used are the seed-heads which follow the equally attractive flowers. Matching the stalks, they, too, are pale green edged with maroon.

If you wish to grow them as pot plants one bulb only in a five-inch pot planted in either October or March is all that is required. Water sparingly from September to March, moderately from March to May and freely afterwards. Apply liquid manure when the flower spike shows. I started growing mine in the greenhouse but decided to move them outside because their large spread of strap-like leaves took up such a lot of room. Mine are now in a sheltered, sunny, well-drained spot in the garden where they seem to have been perfectly happy for the last five years. However, they do need to be protected in the winter by covering with ashes or such-like material.

The unusually shaped container in this design was inspired by the Japanese *usubata*, a traditionally shaped bronze container which they use to hold large and spectacular classical arrangements. My pottery one is glazed pale green with bronze flecks which seems to suit most colour schemes.

Through flower arrangement many of us have extended our hobbies further and for me it has been in the pottery and ceramic sculpture field. Making one's own containers, especially unusual ones like this, is something I can recommend. I was not at all surprised when I read that no less than 200,000 people had enrolled for part-time classes recently in the United Kingdom for this undoubtedly is the best way to begin. In fact, for most people it is the only way as the cost of the necessary equipment these days is so expensive. Since I first started 15 years ago the cost of kilns, potters' wheels and other items has increased four-fold.

Your first lessons will be devoted to getting the feel of clay by making a 'pinch' pot, a simple container made by pinching the clay between thumb and fingers. From this you will progress to 'coiled' pots, then to 'slab-built' containers, until you finally master the art of throwing pots on the wheel. Many of the containers I made in my first year are still firm favourites although they are less than perfect. But, as with everything else, perfection comes with practice. I feel sure that once you have had the satisfaction of arranging in your very own pot you will be inspired to try more ambitious things.

You can't please all the people all the time and I know some people cannot bear to see fresh and dried plant material used together but I am not of that school of thought. As long as the items complement each other and look good I see no reason for not mixing them. In fact in the autumn, when fresh foliage is hard to come by, the use of dried or glycerined material is surely the obvious choice.

These days it is much easier to obtain interesting dried flowers, foliage and seed-heads from abroad than it used to be. Most flower club sales tables have an excellent selection of this type of material. Non-flower club members will have to depend for their purchases on show sales tables, the florist's shop, garden centres and a more recent supplier, the large departmental store where it is often available in the household gifts department. Those lucky enough to travel abroad for their holidays may find some dried leaves or seed-heads to bring home making a useful and evocative souvenir to include in their arrangements. Do remember, however, that the Customs operate stringent restrictions regarding the importation of plants, and rightly so. We have only to think of the accidental introduction of Dutch Elm disease into Great Britain from North America to realize why such regulations are necessary. There is a useful leaflet entitled 'What you should know about Plant Import Regulations' which can be obtained from the Ministry of Agriculture, Fisheries and Food, Eagle House, 90–96 Cannon Street, London EC4N 6HT.

In this design I have used two dried pieces of palm which are a lovely greenish-cream, the colour of the container, and two pieces of pampas grass with the colour impact coming from the magenta spray chrysanthemums which have been grouped together at the base.

Apart from its use in flower arranging, *Cortaderia*, or pampas grass, makes a fine specimen plant in the garden. It should be carefully sited to show off its beauty but at the same time it should be borne in mind that as it matures it will take up quite a considerable amount of room. I planted mine 13 years ago. It was a rather weakly specimen which cost only half a crown and it is now about four feet in diameter and still spreading, so be warned.

There is now a pink pampas on the market but other colours can be obtained with the use of dye. I must admit it is rather a messy job to accomplish but nevertheless worthwhile. The only irritating thing about these gorgeous plumes is that in time they tend to shed their fluff even when they have been sprayed with hair lacquer.

If you grow your own you can avoid this by cutting and glycerining them as soon as they show about three inches of plume emerging from the sheath. They will then last indefinitely and although they are not as fluffy as the dried ones they have a lovely, silky, light tan finish.

With the advent of central heating that old fascinating pastime of seeing faces in the fire has gone but I was reminded of it when making this design as I find I am always seeing faces in my driftwood, too. Mind you, I never seem to see things that others see, and vice versa.

There are, of course, driftwood 'sculptors' about who look at a piece and with a few deft strokes of a chisel and pen-knife transform it into a bird or animal. But most of my collection has been left as nature fashioned it, apart from the necessary cleaning and 'de-bugging'. It seems to have more affinity with flowers that way.

One of my favourite pastimes on holiday walks is vying with my husband to see who can find the best piece and I have to admit that over the past few years he has been the winner. The Lake District has been my most successful hunting ground. There the wood is usually in shades of brown but in Scotland recently I came across whole mountain-sides of beautiful silver-grey wood. There was only enough room in the car to bring one or two pieces home and I was spoilt for choice—an agonizing decision which prompted my husband to suggest that next time we could always hire a removal van!

When collecting wood it is always worthwhile, even with the most splendid find, to cast around and look for a few smaller pieces similarly coloured and grained as the original. Very often you will find that your special piece needs that extra bit to stabilize it for standing or to alter its shape in some way. I have various pieces of wood which are excellent in themselves for smaller arrangements but for show and exhibition work when something larger is needed matching pieces can be attached for additional height.

I try to fasten such wood together by natural means if possible as the use of a fixative is not always reliable. Slotting one piece into another seems to be the best idea. If there is no convenient hole in the heavier piece it is often quite a simple task to make one with a drill and chisel so that the lighter piece of wood can be slotted into it. This sort of assemblage is also much easier to transport about especially when the opening of the boot of the car is on the narrow side. In fact, some enterprising car designer could make a fortune with a specially designed car for the flower arranger with recesses for taking buckets of water and a winch for loading driftwood!

In this design four pieces of similarly grained brown and cream wood have been slotted together into a sculptural shape and I have added a spray of pale lemon chrysanthemums for interest. One or two glycerined laurel leaves strategically placed hide the container.

I suppose I was rather tempting fate by leaving my dahlias to over-winter in the ground these last few years. I have a light, well-drained soil which is helpful in such circumstances and each autumn when I tidied up the garden and cut down the year's growth I used to cover the dahlia bed with it like an eiderdown. Sad to say, a recent ice-age winter put paid to them all. Not one survived.

I know I shall never be able to renew some of my favourites which were given to me by friends as I was never able to identify them even though I have tried at various nurseries and shows. I felt as though I had lost a lot of good friends. Flower arrangers' dahlias are not show dahlias. We like the unusual in shape and colour; none of those giants of the show bench for us. In fact some of my rather puny dahlias would be despised by the exhibitor but they were beloved by me. Still, one has to be an optimist to be a gardener and, who knows, I might even find some I like better. I have already made a start and I must say a couple of new varieties I am growing show promise.

One dahlia, a particular favourite of mine which I never like to be without, is called 'Hugh Mather' after the well-known arranger from St Helens, Merseyside. It is honey-amber in colour and makes a perfect combination with my polished terra-cotta pot. Leaves from the *Yucca recurvifolia* make a bold and long-lasting outline. Two or three thin strips of these leaves have been looped at the front to give it an extra dimension.

As well as my dahlias, my yucca has also been giving me problems. It has not flowered since those two glorious summers of a few years ago. In the first year it produced one mammoth spike of lovely greenish-cream bell-like flowers and the following year it surpassed itself with two glorious spikes. But since then, nothing. I have tried everything to persuade it into flower—even talking to it kindly!—but without success, so I shall just have to go on hoping.

There are three species of this plant which are usually grown in this country. My *Y. recurvifolia*, the *Y. gloriosa* and the *Y. filamentosa*. The latter is sometimes known as 'Adam's needle' and is the one most suitable for small gardens as it requires much less room than the other two. This species, so I am led to believe, flowers frequently after two or three years' growth. The *Y. gloriosa*, on the other hand, does not flower until it is at least five years old.

Even without the flowers it is certainly a handsome plant for the garden. One has to look upon the flower as an added bonus. When mine first flowered I felt as though I had won on the pools!

Some of my flower arrangements come about more by accident than design. Take this one, for example. In this case whilst watering some plants in the greenhouse I carelessly knocked a couple of heads off a salmon-pink *Begonia* and as I cannot bear putting anything on the compost heap which still holds a spark of life they just had to go into an arrangement.

Plumier, the early botanist and monk, was credited with the discovery of this plant in Mexico in 1690. As the plant could not be placed in any known genus he decided to name it after someone he admired—Michael Begon, a French botanist and Governor of Santa Domingo. It was not until the eighteenth century, however, that the first plant arrived at Kew Gardens. There was no real interest in it until the nineteenth century when a shipment from Bolivia came into the hands of James Veitch, a member of the renowned firm of plant growers and distributors. Only when he exhibited them at flower shows both in London and Paris did they catch the public's attention and become popular.

Only recently have I started growing these exotic-looking plants as I have previously fought shy of them, believing that there was some great mystique in producing these splendid show-bench specimens we have all seen. My particular tubers had no special pedigree, in fact not even a name, and were picked up in a local supermarket. And they have not given me a moment's trouble from the time I planted them (hollow side up which, to the unknowing, looks upside-down) to their flowering in great profusion. Happily, the tubers can easily be kept from year to year. As the leaves turn yellow gradually withhold water and dry them off in their pots. For over-wintering they need a temperature of 35–40°F.

I am certainly glad I decided to grow these plants and, indeed, the older I get the more willing I seem to be to try growing new things. The experts with their many ifs and buts do tend to intimidate and consequently discourage rather than encourage experiment. And just to have the same plants growing in the garden and greenhouse year after year is a little unimaginative. After all, we do not keep the same decorations and furniture in the house; we change things about now and then, so why not do so in the garden?

Because *Begonias* are far from ordinary in their looks I wanted an equally unusual outline for them. Eventually, I chose a cascading outline of dried gladioli leaves which had been sprayed ice-blue. Two similarly sprayed clipped palm leaves carry the colour through the design. The twin-funnelled stoneware container is predominantly blue in colour and is standing on a blue lacquered base.

Familiarity breeds contempt in many ways and especially so in gardening. Some of our most common plants rarely merit a second glance by many but I am quite sure that if the self-same plant were a delicate hard-to-grow species it would be marvelled at and written about at length. But I suppose it is the same the world over; what may be exotic to us may only be wild jungle flowers to others!

One of these garden Cinderellas must surely be the ivy (*Hedera*), a great favourite of mine. If you grow several species of these hardy evergreen climbers you will never be without some colourful foliage all the year round.

At first I did not realize that ivy has two different types of growth and now that I do it is another gardening mystery solved. There is the runner growth with lobed leaves and aerial roots for attaching itself for support and the adult growth with wavy margined leaves and no aerial roots which bear the flowers and fruits. This growth is produced from the summit of the runner growth when it reaches the top of the support. Cuttings taken from it will retain the adult form and develop into rounded, bushy shrubs which will flower and fruit freely and are called 'tree ivies'.

In this design I have used both types of growth and they enhance each other admirably. First of all, the angular piece of silver-grey driftwood was impaled on the pin-holder. Following the line of the wood but not hiding it is a piece of the juvenile (or runner) growth whilst a piece of the adult (or arborescent) growth is tucked in at the base and partly overhangs the container. I am not sure which particular species of *Hedera* this is. The leaf is smallish and the variegation is pale yellow which matches perfectly the colour of the spray chrysanthemums. It needed only one stem of these flowers and by cutting judiciously, each with a separate piece of stem, I was able to create this design for the price of this one item.

Ivy lasts wonderfully well when cut and needs no special conditioning procedure except perhaps a swish through soapy water to make sure its leaves are at their glossy best. The ivy, in fact, will probably outlast even the chrysanthemums and these could easily be replaced with other flowers for a change. Two florists' flowers which immediately spring to mind are carnations and roses; either would make a suitable alternative. Nearer Christmas time the addition of some holly with its shiny red berries would make a very suitable design for the festive season. There seems to be no end of possibilities for a simple modern line arrangement such as this.

This design serves to illustrate the point that even the most unpromising pieces of wood can be made to work for you. These two pieces of bleached gorse did not seem to have much potential. However, after some thought and experimentation I was able to use them to create an interesting line taking into account that very important factor— space. Initially, I tried to use them in a low container but their lack of height baulked me every time. The alternative was to try a taller container to gain height and this enabled me to obtain a well-balanced design even with these shortish pieces of wood.

I am always fascinated with all types of driftwood and never ever come back from a walk in the country or along the sea shore without a piece of one sort or another. Some of them languish for years before I find their true potential whilst others adorn an arrangement within a few hours of reaching home. Believe it or not many of my most treasured pieces have been given to me by exasperated flower arrangers who 'can't do a thing with it'. For modern arrangements driftwood is ideal and once you have established an outline with it all that is usually needed is the addition of a couple of flowers. In this instance I have used three acid-yellow fringed cactus dahlias with their own foliage.

The colourful dahlia hails from Mexico where specimens were being cultivated even at the time of the Spanish conquest of that country in 1519. It was not introduced into Europe until 1789 and one of the first seedlings raised was named after Dr Dahl, a Swedish botanist. I am sure he would be astounded to see the vast range of colours and varieties we grow today. And it seems strange to think that this plant's first potential was thought to be as a useful vegetable, like the potato. Edible it might have been but agreeable never and so happily today we have it decorating the table instead of appearing on the menu!

If you only have room in the garden for a few plants it is a good idea to pick a couple of basic colours to fit in with the decor of your home and then plant pompons, medium decoratives and cactus varieties within your colour range. You will find this much more useful than having a haphazard collection.

Dahlias last quite well in arrangements provided they are fresh to start with and have been well conditioned. I give them the boiling water treatment (previously mentioned) and then they have a long drink overnight before being arranged next day. An aspirin added to the water will discourage the formation of algae which is sometimes a problem with these flowers.

This particular piece of ivy wood has only just come into its own as outline material although it has been used many times previously the other way up. Consequently, its fascinating outline was usually obscured somewhat with plant material. What is now the apex of the outline used to be its base. In those days there was an additional two inches of wood above the apex which used to anchor the wood on to the pin-holder. As this now ruined the shape it was removed with saw and chisel and part of it was glued back on to improve its profile. You will see it in its original form in the Winter section of the book giving an outline to a design featuring some of my beloved ivy. I think you will agree when you compare the two that this is a much more effective way of using it.

I sometimes think that because we are preoccupied with looking for an easy means to anchor the wood we tend to forget about getting its best possible outline and this is a typical example of what I mean. So do consider your own pieces of wood from all angles and experiment with them and maybe you will find that what you thought was just ordinary had now become extraordinary because of a little extra thought.

This very original container was given to me by Jean Taylor and has become one of my favourites for modern arranging. It is a coil-built stoneware pot glazed with greyish-brown markings and is very heavy indeed which makes it ideal for large arrangements. Its shape reminds me of many things, from spinning discs to bracket fungi. It certainly isn't the easiest pot in which to arrange flowers as its inside shape causes problems with one's mechanics. For this design I filled it with old floral foam which was solidly compacted so that it would not disintegrate when this heavy wood was inserted into it.

The two lovely chrysanthemum blooms are, so my florist tells me, 'Orange Moors'. They are light tan with yellow reflex petals and give an attractive bold highlight to the arrangement. It stands nearly four feet high and so these flowers are of ideal proportions; anything smaller would have ruined the scale of the design.

Scale is such an important part of design and one, I feel, that is not stressed enough. Not only should all the plant material be to scale but the container and accessories should be as well. Like me, you must have seen many excellent exhibits at shows downpointed because the accessory used had been completely out of scale with the rest of the exhibit. And because of this single factor what might have been a prize-winner becomes an also-ran.

This fascinating swirling outline can easily be made by anyone with access to a weeping willow. You will need several branches about 6–8 feet long with their attendant whip-like smaller shoots. I have never found difficulty in stripping the bark from these branches provided it is done soon after they have been cut. If this is not possible they should be left soaking in water as it is vitally important that the branches should be kept supple to enable you to strip them successfully. You will find that the thicker parts of the branches can be stripped quite quickly but do not rush it when you get to the finer stems. They break easily and a little haste at this stage can ruin everything as it is virtually impossible to glue such fine stems together again. Whilst the stems are full of sap and still supple tie them into your preconceived patterns before leaving them to dry out. When they are dry leave them for at least a couple of weeks then untie the coils and gently tease them into interesting swirling curves. Care should be taken as the dried stems will now be rather brittle and can easily break. Nevertheless, these unusual outlines will last for years provided you are careful.

The outline for this design was made from three separate branches, two long and one short. The two longer pieces were intertwined for the top part and the shorter piece, lower right, was slotted upwards between their stems to give depth to the outline. The ideal container for this type of arrangement is one with funnel openings which dispenses with the use of any mechanics. It is simply a case of wedging all the materials tightly into one funnel and leaving the other empty for topping up with water.

The main part of this container is slab-built with only the two funnels thrown on the wheel. It was dipped in a pale lemon glaze and then sprayed with a mixture of copper and iron oxides. When fired it turned out to be a delightful greenish colour with brownish highlights and seems to complement any colour of flower. It is perfect for these pale blue hydrangeas which have a greenish tinge. I have inserted the leaves on separate stems as they seem to last better that way. You will find with these flowers that the more mature they are the longer they will last. Try at the same time to cut them on a piece of old wood. Either float or stand them up to their necks in water overnight before arranging. An occasional damping with a mist spray when arranged will help to prolong their life.

Hydrangeas will dry beautifully and easily for your winter arrangements. Simply cut them when they have a papery feel, stand them in a jar with an inch of water and dry them off slowly in a warm atmosphere. Done this way they will retain their colour well.

Dahlias are excellent flowers for modern designs. Their clear bright colours coupled with the geometric precision of their petals seem just right. And two lovely 'My Love' white cactus dahlias sparked off this design. They reminded me of those 'shooting-star' type of firework and so this was to be my theme. And here I have to admit to a child-like delight in any firework display; I just can't resist them.

With a theme such as this my problem was how to get a flower in space and in water at the same time! But to any flower arranger worth her salt 'a problem posed is a problem solved' so I decided the answer was to use a piece of finger-thick rattan. Luckily, it had already been made into this orbital shape and was painted black—just what I wanted. The next thing to consider was a suitable container and for this I chose one in shiny black incised with a suitable motif which had a funnel-type aperture for flowers. This would obviate any problems posed by a container with a pin-holder which would have to be hidden in some way.

First of all, the cane was slotted tightly into the funnel of the container and the lower white flower happily fitted into the 'V' made by the two ends of the rattan. Next, where the two loops of the outline met I taped a black lipstick top to hold water for the elevated flower. And to complete my idea I had in some way to depict the tails of the 'shooting stars'. For this I chose two black-painted skeletonized palmetto palms which I invisibly wired below each flower.

It is often more fun thinking out a theme for the arrangements in your home rather than just working purely on design, especially if you do not exhibit in shows where this kind of work is done. There is nothing more stultifying to one's own creativity than doing the same type of arrangement constantly as it becomes almost a part of the wallpaper rather than an entity in itself. Some idea or theme expressed purely with plant material and without the aid of any accessories can be quite an invigorating challenge.

By the same token, vary the places in your home where you have your arrangements and occasionally depart from the norm. If you usually go in for traditional arrangements because you feel they fit in with your type of decor then try something different. You need not be too adventurous and do something totally abstract which would look incongruous but something half-way; say, a modern line-design. You will surprise everybody—even yourself!

One of the drawbacks for exhibitors who do modern designs at shows is that if they are good they are long remembered and so cannot be repeated. Although a case of 'once seen, never forgotten' is, I suppose, a compliment. On the other hand with the more traditional triangle this precept does not apply. This self-same style can be done *ad nauseam* and no-one will ever cry 'I've seen it before!' as they do with very imaginative modern designs. This is possibly why modern arranging with its 'one-off' exhibits is such an interesting and absorbing facet of this hobby of ours.

Striving to be different all the time is a great challenge and I have to admit it can be a little exhausting at times. One sometimes finds ideas for exploration in the most unlikely places far from the obvious initial source of inspiration of garden and countryside. And many of mine have come from such a source at home.

We live in a house built about 1890 with a spacious set of basement rooms. When the previous owners left these rooms—with our agreement—were not cleared out as my husband and I had already noticed some interesting items we would be happy to inherit. It turned out to be an Aladdin's Cave where flower arranging treasures abounded, from tree-felling axes which eventually featured in a 'Forresters' Arms' inn sign exhibit to an old oil lamp used in a 'Harvest Table' class. Even after 15 years I still seem to find just what I want down there and it has become the source of many a wry comment by flower arranging friends of mine.

The main basement room now houses my pottery. A solid 15-foot-long bench, part of which is covered with slate, is another inherited treasure. This makes an ideal working surface for making my slab-built containers, one of which I have used in this arrangement. It is roughly crescent-shaped and is raised on a similarly shaped base.

The larder shelf was my source of inspiration for the design itself. The buff-coloured spaghetti, I decided, would go beautifully with this cream pot which I had recently made and not so far used. I grouped about a third of a packet of the spaghetti together and slipped an elastic band round the bottom to keep the strands together. Had I been using dried plant material I could easily have impaled them as they were on to the pin-holder but as I wanted to use fresh flowers they would have to be kept out of the water. I eventually found a bottle top which I was able to fasten on to the pin-holder and this solved the problem. Just one spray of 'Nicolette', a biscuit-coloured single chrysanthemum, was all that was needed to complete the design.

This same idea could also be effectively carried out with a bunch of decapitated green rushes which are plentiful in most damp spots in the countryside.

WINTER

WINTER is the season of the year when flowers are scarce in the garden and expensive in the shops—and it is the time when your pot plants come into their own. Not only are they beautiful in their own right but they can often supply you with those few flowers or leaves for a special arrangement.

The use of indoor plants has increased enormously over the last decade and so has the variety available. A visit to many a chain store, supermarket or garden centre will present you with a mind-boggling array and you will be spoilt for choice. However, your selection is made much easier for practically all the plants are named with their species and their own particular growing instructions. If you are inexperienced it is always better to start with the easier ones and when you have gained some expertise move on to the more difficult species.

Among the easiest to grow are the *Chlorophytum* (spider plant), *Cissus Antarctica* (kangaroo vine), *Ficus elastica* (rubber plant), *Hedera* (Ivy), *Monstera deliciosa* (Swiss cheese plant), *Rhoicissus rhomboidea* (grape ivy), *Sanseveria* (mother-in-law's tongue), and the ever-popular *Tradescantia* (wandering Jew).

It is always a challenge to grow successfully some of the more difficult plants so here are a few suggestions: *Aechmea, Anthurium, Aphelandra* (zebra plant), *Begonia rex, Codiaeum* (croton), *Dracaena, Dieffenbachia* (dumb cane) and that delightful fern, the *Nephrolepsis*.

As with flower arranging you should consider the colour and shapes of your plants so they will enhance their new environment. The croton, for example, will provide a dramatic splash of colour in a simple style of room while the lovely cascading greenery of the *Nephrolepsis* will complement a room which is more brightly decorated. In a more spacious room nothing could be more dramatic than a large plant of tree-like proportions such as *Ficus benjamina* (the weeping fig) or the *Howea* which was formerly known as the Kentia palm.

But do look after them. There is nothing worse than having a half-dead flower arrangement in a room and the same can be said about pot plants. They should be clean and healthy and bursting with vitality to look their best. A little careful grooming can make a jaded plant soon look in tip-top condition, so keep their leaves clean with an occasional wipe, carefully trim any damaged leaves and remove any yellowing ones. You will be amazed what a difference such attention to detail can make.

For this design I took two flowers from an *Anthurium scherzerianum* which is the easiest species of this particular plant to grow. The *A. andreanum*, the popular one seen at flower shows is much more demanding and requires a constant warm and humid atmosphere. The flowers with their palette-shaped spathes of brilliant scarlet and a spiral orange-red spadix are so dramatic I decided to use them on their own without any foliage. A beautifully textured piece of driftwood was all that was needed to set them off in this greenish-bronze container.

This design was just done for fun with some left-over plant materials. As I have previously confessed, I find it hard to throw away anything that still has a spark of life left in it so this is really a 'botanical doodle'.

There is something about the iris leaf that captivates me as it always seems to have such potential for experimentation where flower arranging is concerned. It can be manipulated into many shapes; it can be threaded or shredded and it can be clipped at various angles.

These leaves are from the *Iris pseudacorus* (wild flag iris) and because of its invasive nature I grow it in a large sunken sink at the bottom of the garden to keep it within bounds. It will grow quite successfully in the border but if you want to have leaves up to 5 feet in height they need to have their feet in water. And although I do not often use their yellow flowers I find their large green seed pods an unusual addition to my arrangements. Its more glamorous sister, the *I. pseudacorus* 'Variegata', graces my garden pool where its glorious yellow striped leaves are supreme before flowering when the stripes slowly fade.

The two thick green stems on which the long iris leaf is impaled are from the *Iris sibirica*, another species well worth growing, with smaller flowers in either white or varying shades of blue. They, too, provide interesting seed-heads which can be used fresh, dried or glycerined. These plants are easy to grow in any open situation with reasonably fertile soil and, happily for the arranger, spread quite quickly.

The final item for this all-green arrangement consists of four heads from the *Cyperus* (umbrella plant) which grows with gay abandon in various parts of the garden where it has seeded itself.

Where and how to start is the most difficult thing in a design such as this. Artists admit to being intimidated by the blank canvas as do writers with the blank page. The first stroke, so to speak, is the most difficult but once you have made it you are away. So get something 'down' even if it has to be altered later. This very act will bring forth ideas and it is then a matter of adding and subtracting different materials until the finished design is pleasing to the eye.

Although one must bear in mind all the principles of good design, do not be enslaved by them. Have courage to experiment. Try, for example, to have the highlight of your design at the top instead of in the more usual position at the base. Experiment, too, with balance; abandon symmetry and be more adventurous. As long as your design has equal 'eye-pull' on either side of your imaginary central axis it will have the balance you are striving for.

At first glance you might wonder what an arrangement featuring roses is doing in the Winter section of this book. The answer is that it is not quite what it seems. Only the rose foliage is fresh; the roses are made of silk. Thankfully, I have no hang-ups about using silk or paper flowers in my arrangements though I draw the line very firmly at plastic except at Christmas, of course, when they are invaluable. Some of these silk flowers are well worth having in stock for times when flowers are scarce or too expensive. They are not cheap but as they last for ever they make a good investment.

The great secret with artificial and dried arrangements in general is not to leave them in your room until they become too familiar. It is the ephemeral quality of flowers that makes arrangements so beguiling so remember this with your dried arrangements. Try rearranging them or even putting them away for a while so that they do not lose their impact.

Fasciated forsythia makes an unusual outline for this design. I never cease to marvel at the sculptural form this fasciation takes. At home and at shows it is always a talking point as it does not appear to be known to many other than flower arrangers. It is still rather hard to find, possibly because of its limited growth, but it is worth seeking out. I have half a dozen pieces which can be used separately or put together for one magnificent outline. The stems are very hard indeed; in fact, they seem almost fossilized and so I usually put them on some sort of false stem to facilitate easier fixing on to the pin-holder. It is a good idea to use the same principle with the roses as their plastic-covered wire stems are also hard to fix on the pin-holder.

I am sure you will agree that these flowers are very naturalistic. The foliage, however, is a little disappointing and does not seem anything like the real thing. After all, there is an affinity between the delicate rose petals and silk but not much between silk and the tougher texture of rose leaves. No doubt this is why I was a little disappointed with the result when I first tried out these flowers. The addition of fresh foliage made all the difference and although I did not set out to deceive most people have been taken-in and complimented me on my out-of-season roses!

The brown of the forsythia and the tan of the terra-cotta pot made an excellent foil for these apricot-coloured 'blooms'. The two bamboo mats have been added to improve the balance of the design. The top wood is visually heavy and so the additional weight added by the base makes it a more pleasing composition.

Whoever coined the name 'Bird of Paradise' for the *Strelitzia reginae* was certainly inspired. To see them growing in profusion amid their majestic leaves these orange and blue flowers look for all the world like the crest on the head of some exotic bird. With their thick straight stems and angular shape they are not the easiest flowers to arrange. They present a challenge to any flower arranger lucky enough to have bought or been given some. Often the flowers only are available without the leaves which again adds to that challenge.

Because of their size an equally impressive container needs to be used otherwise they can easily make your arrangement appear top-heavy. For my design I chose this sculptural stoneware container which is very heavy and therefore very stable. These particular flowers, along with one leaf, were brought back for me by a friend from a holiday in Madeira where, she tells me, they are in season throughout the year. And whilst I had no difficulty placing the three flowers, the single leaf caused rather a problem and although I tried all the possibilities I was not happy with any of them. The simple answer came with a sudden inspiration—why not cut the leaf in two with a sharp knife down its midrib? This I did quite satisfactorily and it did not seem to affect the life of the leaf at all.

Mechanics for this container are difficult and my easiest solution was to pack it tightly with old wet floral foam which would hold these rather heavy flowers securely.

When you come to arrange *Strelitzias* you will notice that the angle of the flowers to the stem is not always the same. I was able to use one with a lesser angle at the top for the upward movement I wanted and the other two more acutely angled ones were used lower in the design. My two half-leaves deceived everyone and helped to give the design a good balance. An attractive piece of driftwood was hooked on to the lip of the container which gave added interest at this point.

These splendid flowers last well in water and often extra flowers can be teased out of the 'beak' as the original ones die back. They are still worth keeping even when they are dead for although they lose their colour they do not lose their unusual shape. The leaves as they die take on a most attractive colour and contort into fascinating shapes.

Strelitzias can be grown in this country in a heated greenhouse provided you have the room they require. I have two friends who grow them satisfactorily in the house although they do not flower as often as they would do in a greenhouse where a humid atmosphere could be maintained. One day recently when I called to see one of them I was amazed to see the plant with half a dozen beautiful flowers. It was not until I had a closer look that I realized how realistic silk *Strelitzia* flowers really are!

When looking at black and white photographs of other people's fresh flower arrangements I can readily visualize them in colour but with dried arrangements I tend to see them only in shades of brown. Which is a great pity as colour plays an important part in many of them.

Take this design, for example. Unless you had seen it in colour and knew otherwise it appears to be in browns and fawns. However, the introduction of two shining, burnt-orange coloured Japanese palm fans and tall grasses of the same hue bring it to life and give it more impact than a completely brown monochromatic design would have done. So do not shrink from introducing some of the artificially coloured materials which abound in the shops these days—but use them with discretion.

These two fronds are from the *Cycas*, sometimes called the sago palm. The larger of the two has been preserved in glycerine and is golden brown in colour while the lower leaf is dried and a pale fawn shade. If you get the opportunity, do buy the glycerined variety as they can be manipulated into curving shapes. The dried ones, although useful, are very brittle and soon get damaged. The two giant 'powder puffs' are the central boss of the seed-heads of the *Cynara cardunculus* (cardoon) and carefully kept intact with hair-spray. They are oatmeal in colour and have a lovely silky texture.

If you want to grow something different in your herbaceous border why not try the cardoon? Not only does it provide these lovely seed-heads but it grows up to six feet tall, has three-foot long, deeply serrated, grey leaves and makes a majestic addition to any garden. Moreover, its thistle-like flowers are more beautiful and more thistle-like than the *Onopordum* (Scottish heraldic thistle) itself and you have the tantalizing choice of using them fresh or leaving them to dry.

The cardoon is a near-relation of the globe artichoke and if it is grown in a trench its blanched stalks and the midribs of its leaves can be used as a vegetable. It has a delicious 'nutty' flavour—so I am told. Personally, I have never tasted it. As a flower arranger this would be akin to eating one's pet rabbit!

Mechanics for dried arrangements are always simple as there is no water problem. For modern designs such as this when there are few materials to be fixed I still try to use a pin-holder which can easily be concealed with a few pebbles. If, however, the stems are unsuitable for this method of fixing, a small piece of floral foam (there is a special brown kind for use with dried materials) fixed on to an appropriate holder will do the trick. This will have to be hidden by the strategic placement of leaves or other suitable materials. Even though it might be invisible when viewed from the front it will surely be seen from the sides so make sure you have done this—or you will soon learn about it from your flower-arranging friends!

I recently read in *The Garden*, the journal of the Royal Horticultural Society, a very interesting and informative report on 'The Ivy Trial'. The only previous study of this plant was carried out in 1889/90 at the Society's garden in Chiswick, and it says much for its present popularity that it should be chosen again for such a study in depth.

It is one of my favourite foliages and I have already extolled its virtues along with the naming of a selection which I grow very successfully in my garden. One of the joys of ivy is that it is so easy to propagate. A small piece will soon root and grow sufficiently well to cut trails from in a couple of years' time. Some of my best ivies have been grown in this way and I am always on the look out for new ones.

Not only is the fresh ivy useful but so is the dead! This vertical piece was stripped off a felled tree and makes an interesting outline for this type of arrangement. A second piece of wood has been placed to rest on the rim of the container and three separate pieces of *Hedera colchica* 'Variegata' were added to complete the picture.

This type of design will last for weeks and indeed almost for ever if you have a suitable potted ivy to use instead. In fact, you could make a pot-et-fleur of it by adding a few seasonal flowers to give extra impact. Mind you, I am quite happy with the foliage alone especially when it is as beautiful as this.

There are many other evergreen shrubs that could be used in a similar way and one that immediately springs to mind is the *Euonymus fortunei* 'Silver Queen' with its broad variegated leaves of green and white. Alternatively, the *Griselina littoralis* 'Variegata', a slightly tender evergreen species which has leathery lustrous yellow and green leaves, would be an excellent substitute. Another shrub rather neglected in the past but given a new lease of life by flower arrangers who value it for its own particular beauty is the *Aucuba japonica* 'Maculata' (the spotted laurel). When seen by the roadside covered with grime it is not a particularly pretty sight but swish it about in some soapy water and it positively glows. It reminds me of those advertisements for certain bath salts where a poor dishevelled person enters the bathroom only to emerge fresh and glowing in a short space of time—such is the *Aucuba*.

The three shrubs which I have mentioned have all been grown from cuttings begged from friends. This is something I find very rewarding not just because I have a plant 'for free' but it makes it more interesting to have known its own particular antecedents. Gathering one's own seed, too, for later sowing has a similar feel about it and one I find very satisfying.

There is something about the velvet faces of the anemones with their lovely black centres which is especially captivating. Their colour, too, in shades of red and purple, adds to their rich and glowing appeal. Though to see them tightly bunched together in a bucket at the florist's is enough to put you off them altogether. They have little appeal alongside their more glamorous neighbours. But they soon respond to that nice long overnight drink and the warmth of the home and show themselves to their best advantage—almost like humans!

Another name for the anemone is the windflower, from the Greek *anemos* meaning wind, a reference to their chosen habitat in exposed places. *Anemone caronaria* (the Poppy anemone) originated in Asia Minor and two descendants from this species are the most popular strains of florists' anemones today—'De Caen', the single variety, and 'St Brigid', a double or semi-double strain.

In the right situation anemones can easily be grown in the garden. Their wants are simple—a well-drained soil in full sun. By successive plantings they can produce flowers almost all the year round. Plant the corms at a depth of two inches and you will find that the larger ones take about three months to flower whilst smaller ones will take up to six months. For winter flowering it is a good idea to protect them with cloches from October onwards. I grew some quite successfully some years ago in a bed which was raised to improve the drainage—a tip worth remembering if your soil is heavy.

My pottery container is rather unusual and it is to my own design. It was made by utilizing two plaster bats. These are flat plaster shapes made to stand pottery on whilst it is drying. The special property of the plaster is that when dry it will act like a sponge drawing water out of any clay that rests upon it. These bats can easily be made by pouring plaster of Paris into a metal pie dish which has been treated with size. When the plaster has set they can be removed and are ready for use. To make this container I rolled out some clay, just like pastry, but to an even thickness of three-eighths of an inch. Cutting it in two I then eased the clay carefully over the two reversed bats, trimming the edges before leaving them to dry. After several hours they had reached the 'leather-hard' stage when it is possible to handle clay without it losing its shape. First, I cut a star-shaped opening at the centre of one of the rounds before joining them both together. Three small feet were then attached to the base before it was biscuit-fired and then glazed a rich peacock-blue.

The colour of this container seems to enhance further the rich colour of the anemones which were grouped together at the base of a piece of my beloved driftwood.

A glowing array of *Gerberas* seen in a flower shop on a winter's day is a heart-warming sight. These lovely flowers, natives of South Africa, are imported into this country from Guernsey, Holland and Israel so that we now have them for our flower arrangements all the year round.

There is nothing unusual about their daisy-like appearance but it is their range of colours that set them apart—white, cream, yellow, orange-pink, crimson and purple. And as well as the singles there are also some fascinating double-flowered varieties to choose from.

In Great Britain these half-hardy and tender perennial plants normally require greenhouse cultivation although in the mild, sheltered areas of the south and west they might just survive in the open. Seeds should be sown in pots or pans of seed compost in February or March at a temperature of 61°–64°F (16°–18°C). When large enough to handle the seedlings should be transferred into boxes and later still into 3½–4-inch pots of growing compost or into their flowering positions if outdoors. In summer, in the greenhouse, water them freely and give ample ventilation, shading them lightly from May to September. Once established the plants can over-winter at a temperature of 41°–45°F (5°–7°C). Keep the plants just moist at all times and they can be divided annually in March. If you wish to chance them outdoors they seem happiest in ordinary, well-drained garden soil in a sunny sheltered position at the foot of a wall. Remember to cut faded flower stems down to ground level to prolong flowering.

When selecting *Gerberas* at your flower shop do choose them with care or you might be disappointed. See that the flowers have straight stems and non-mouldy centres. These flowers have a tendency to flop and a little care taken with their conditioning may hopefully prevent this happening. When you get them home remove the plastic cone used for packing, cut the stem end, burn in a flame for about half a minute and then place at once in a container of deep tepid water. If you can leave them like this in the dark for two days all the better, but at least 24 hours' preparation should be given.

These three pink *Gerberas* were a present from Sylvia, my local florist. What a treat it is these days to find someone as helpful as she is. No matter how bizarre or outlandish my demands may be it seems I only have to ask and whether it is something out of season or a rare species, if it can be obtained it will be.

Grey is an excellent complement for pink in flower arrangements so I have chosen a container, a marvellously shaped piece of *Manzanita* wood and a dried piece of palm, all in shades of grey. Anchoring wood safely often causes problems but luckily this piece had a convenient hole at the base which enabled me to impale it on to the pin-holder with a short thick piece of teasel stem firmly wedged through it. When the curved piece of palm was added it only needed the three flowers to highlight the design and in this setting they positively glowed.

This beautifully proportioned pot with its simple leaf motif hardly needs any embellishments but to the flower arranger it presents a challenge. How can its beauty be further enhanced without taking the eye away from the container itself? Colourful flowers, I felt, would be the wrong choice as they would dominate the design. I eventually decided upon an arrangement of these lovely dried leaves from the *Iris ochroleuca* which I have already mentioned elsewhere in the book.

The procedure for achieving this design is very simple—I cut the leaves when they are at their peak and by gently stroking them persuade them into interesting curves. I then assemble the leaves in my left hand with my right and when I am satisfied with the design I carefully place it on a pin-holder to dry. The unblemished leaves will gradually dry a beautiful biscuit colour and if handled carefully will last indefinitely.

For this design I integrated the leaves from two separate pre-dried outlines. When they were assembled to my satisfaction I whipped a piece of Sellotape round the bottom to keep them in place. The mechanics—which are always a problem with modern designs—could not be easier. I simply used dried sand which was poured into the pot until it nearly reached the top. The leaves were then inserted into it for about an inch and to the casual observer they would seem to be held in place by magic. It is much easier using sand for a pot with a narrow neck than floral foam. Although it would do the job just as well it is a time-consuming job extracting it afterwards. If, however, you wanted to use dried leaves such as these with fresh flowers they should be fastened on to a false stem so they will stand proud of the water. I find the teasel ideal for supplying me with all the false stems I need. If you grow mammoth specimens, as I do, the stems will vary depending upon the part of the plant from which they are taken. Very useful fine stems about $\frac{1}{4}$-inch thick can be cut from the top of the plant and sturdy one-inch-thick pieces from the base. They are useful in both their fresh and dried state.

Being a potter myself I naturally have a great interest in other people's pots and this one, made at a local pottery, completely captivated me. As well as its perfect proportions and its simple decoration, its glaze is stunning. This was obtained by reduction-firing and is something which can only be done if you have a fuel-burning kiln as it is necessary to cut down on the air supply for chemical inter-action to take place within the kiln. With an electric kiln such as mine, such experiments unfortunately are not practical; hence my admiration for those who can use this technique.

Most flower arrangers are impulsive buyers of unconsidered trifles—bits and pieces of junk, bric-à-brac, and the like which whilst attractive in themselves do not immediately suggest a way in which they can be used. These two brown and cream straw fans which I picked up in the sales are a good example. Not until now have I found a satisfactory way of incorporating them into an arrangement.

Delving among my collection of dried materials looking for something bold and complementary I came across two glycerined leaves of the fan palm (*Tachycarpus*) and some lovely tan-coloured, curled and dried leaves given to me on the tragic death of a friend's rubber plant.

Now that I had decided upon the materials the next step was to incorporate them into a bold arrangement. The idea of having a palm leaf and a fan placed high in the design appealed to me and at the same time posed a problem. A false stem of some kind seemed to be the answer and it had to be a part of the design at the same time as it could be easily seen if viewed from either side. A further search in my boxes revealed a large and beautifully coloured and textured piece of dried *Angelica* which would fit the bill admirably. First of all, the stem was impaled on to the heavy pin-holder which I had placed on a dark brown suede-covered block of wood. I then slotted the top palm leaf into its hollow stem. The fan (with a thick wire slipped up its bound handle) was easily pinned into the thick stem at the correct angle. Finally, to complete the design, the rest of the chosen materials, including two giant, orangey-red, paper poppies, were inserted on to the pin-holder with their own stems.

If you have not grown the majestic *Angelica* in your garden you are certainly missing something which is not only attractive but useful in many ways. These plants are biennials so set the seed on two consecutive years so that you will have flowers each successive year thereafter and, indeed, for evermore as they are very prolific self-seeders. In fact, you will be able to supply all your friends and neighbours with them and still have some over for the compost heap. They are not fussy about the soil or position in the garden as long as they have room to grow to a height of 6–10 feet. In May and June they are a glorious sight with their rounded umbels of tiny yellow-green flowers held high on bold green stems with their pale green aromatic leaves. The plants will slowly die back after flowering and produce seed, when the dried stems and heads can be harvested for future use. Not only can they be used in their natural state, they can also be painted very successfully. At Christmas time they look very dramatic when painted white and glittered for that extra sparkle.

And for those with a culinary bent wishing to practise a little one-upmanship, you can amaze your friends by producing your very own crystallized angelica!

Here is another design featuring *Gerberas* where the dark outline and dark container serve to emphasize the bright pink of the flowers. To soften the outline a little so that it is less stark two pieces of *Asparagus plumosus* have been added. This fern is popular with *Ikebana* enthusiasts but seldom used in western-type arrangements. Its branched stems reminded me in some way of the skeletal form of the two dead branches and so it seemed an appropriate material to incorporate into the design. The tall branch with its additional placement hooked on to it is blackthorn whilst the more angular bolder piece, fixed on to the container, is hawthorn.

Whilst beachcombing in North Wales I came upon the latter piece which by its shape suggests it is from a hedge which had been layered. The blackthorn was found on a winter walk down the lanes of the Wirral Peninsula where I live. Incidentally, one of the best times for finding interestingly shaped branches is in the winter when the trees are bare and there are no leaves to obscure their shapes.

Some branches well worth seeking out are those from the common alder which is usually found by ponds and streams or other damp places. It has cone-like black female catkins which remain on the tree throughout the winter, as do the clusters of small cones on the sweeping branches of the larch. Both are most useful as outline material. Another two items worth gathering, in old gloves if possible, are pieces of burnt heather and gorse. Choose the more dramatic, thick, twisted pieces if possible as they lend themselves better to modern designs. As well as branches you will find other treasure trove on a winter's walk: tall dry grasses, for example, or wild dock and sometimes lovely dried stems of hogweed and teasel. That 'seeing eye' which all flower arrangers should cultivate is essential on trips like these.

Your own garden, too, can be a happy hunting ground in the winter months. The fascinating silhouettes of the branches of the *Salix matsudana* 'Tortuosa' and *Corylus contorta* against the sky will enable you to select their best branches for cutting. Even when tidying up the garden be selective in what you throw away. Keep all useful dried stems from plants such as *Kniphofia*, angelica, *Inula*, *Bocconia* and *Miscanthus*. And when it comes to seed-heads those from the *Acanthus*, *Hosta sieboldiana* 'Elegans', iris, poppy, teasel and cardoon will all make useful items for your dried arrangements.

Some of the most mundane material can be made into fascinating outlines with a little ingenuity as, for example, my latest creation made simply from dried angelica stalks which can be seen in colour plate 2. One large piece of stem was split in half and from it I cut out a number of 4 × 1-inch-wide pieces which were assembled in three fan-shaped sections. Two of these were inserted into a two-foot piece of stem, one at the top and the other let into the stem a third of the way down while the third had a separate stem of its own. Painted black it makes an original outline for a modern design.

That old flower arranging adage 'If in doubt leave it out' is particularly apt where modern arrangements are concerned. The fewer components used the better—a clean-cut and tailored look arrests the eye more so than the over-ornamented.

For this design I have selected just three types of material—dramatic foliage, unusual flowers and interesting seed-heads. The *Iris ochroleuca* has provided me with its lovely biscuit-coloured leaves to give height to the arrangement. The unusual dried flowers are from the *Heliconia humilis* which is sometimes known as 'Lobster Claws', and what a perfect description that is. When they are in full bloom their claw-like bracts are bright lobster-red in colour. When dried they lose a lot of their impact but, nevertheless, their unusual form still catches the eye even though they are now tan and cream. For the seed-heads I have chosen two silky-cream powder-puffs from the central box of the cardoon (*Cynara cardunculus*).

Many arrangers do not seem to be aware of the source of these lovely powder-puffs. They throw their dried cardoon and artichoke flowers away because they are beginning to disintegrate, not realizing that if they stripped off the outer bracts carefully and then gently plucked off the mauve centres of the flowers this is what they would find—the capitulum. They have to be handled very carefully as they are extremely brittle and break easily. Spray them heavily with hair lacquer and this will prolong their life. Another hazard with these heads is that more often than not they will break away from their stems. The hard round disc left is difficult to fasten on to another stem. After a lot of experimenting I have now found a satisfactory solution to this problem and an easy one, too. Find an old wooden cotton reel and saw it into ½-inch-thick sections. Fix one of these sections with impact adhesive to the hard round base of the powder-puff and it is now a simple matter to fix a false stem into the hole of the cotton reel. This also has another great advantage which I did not at first realize in that it enables me to store the seed-heads flat in a box and so prevent them being damaged as they could so easily be if they were stored in the normal way. When they are required I simply add the necessary false stem (usually teasel), straight or curved, whichever I require for my design. Incidentally, I have successfully dyed some of these powder-puffs in orange vegetable dye used for cake decoration and others I have coloured with car touch-up aerosol paint.

I chose a favourite terra-cotta pot for this design to harmonize with the tan, fawn and cream colour scheme. All the dried materials were impaled on a pin-holder which was hidden from view with some brown and tan pieces of flint. And because this design is quite tall for the size of the container two bamboo rafts have been placed beneath it to improve the visual balance.

For this arrangement I have to thank a flower-arranger friend who brought me these lovely cymbidium orchids back from a holiday in Madeira. It brightened up a cheerless wintry day and as they are such long-lasting flowers I was able to enjoy their beauty for several weeks afterwards.

I have always considered these exotics of the plant world as being something only for the experts to grow but recently I have been tempted to have a go myself after reading a persuasive piece on their cultivation in the home. At one time the cost was the main deterrent to buying them but today they compare very favourably in price with other of the more sophisticated pot-plants. Apparently, the most important of the orchid's needs is plenty of light (at least ten hours a day in the growing period) coupled with moist air. If you can supply these two essentials then a visit to an orchid nursery would be worthwhile for specialist advice on the type which grows best in your own particular environment.

Orchids are such eye-catchers that only two or three are needed for an arrangement. For a delightful dining-table decoration try integrating them, in their tubes, into a grouping of fruit on a flat glass or silver dish. They look equally attractive in conjunction with a small grouping of coral and iridescent shells which you may have brought back from a sun-baked holiday beach as a happy souvenir. And taking a tip from their natural habitat, you will find that they blend beautifully in a design where they have been skilfully positioned about a polished piece of silver-grey driftwood. They may seem an extravagance but they are a good investment for the busy hostess when time is at a premium as they can be arranged well in advance. Another advantage is that they will take up little room on the table where the food should take pride of place.

From all this you might think that orchids are strictly for small arrangements but this is not the case at all as you can see from this three-foot-high design which is based on a short spray of cymbidium orchids. For the outline I chose three pieces of bleached *Edgeworthia* 'Mitsumata'. This very useful material from Japan can often be found on sale at some of the larger shows at the floral accessory stalls. I have even seen it at garden centres as well as in large stores where they sell selections of dried plant materials.

The 'Mitsumata' always needs cutting and trimming before use as it looks rather ragged in its imported state. For this design I cut about three inches from the top of each piece and sanded them down to make a smoothly rounded end. The tall upright one was impaled on to the pin-holder whilst the second and third pieces were slotted through it to make a pleasing, well-balanced outline. Finally, the stem of orchids was added and the pink of the flowers combined well with the pale green of the slab-built container.

That symbol of sunshine, the palm tree, can only be grown in this country in the more favoured areas which is a great pity as it provides such wonderful foliage for flower arrangements.

Rarely have I had the chance of using these splendid leaves fresh but, happily, dried ones can be purchased in this country if you hunt around for them. Over the years I have been able to acquire quite a selection of different types of this species and find their unusual forms very eye-catching in a variety of different ways.

You might not realize that there is any connection between two of the items displayed in this design—the fan palm and the rattan—but there is. The rattan comes from the *Calamus maximus* (the rattan palm), a species which grows extensively in the higher altitudes of tropical South-East Asia, Malaysia, the Philippines, Borneo, Java and Sumatra. They are seldom grown commercially and are harvested from the wild. The pliable stems of this palm scramble up to 200 feet into the tops of surrounding trees and cling to them by means of hooks on their pinnate leaves. It must be a dangerous job cutting it down in the jungle because in its natural state it is covered with vicious thorns which have to be removed before it goes to market. Depending on its use, the rattan is then machine-cut to various thicknesses for the manufacture of furniture, trays, baskets and bags.

The rattan we buy in the shops for our arrangements varies in diameter from very thin to finger-thick. As a general rule the thicker the rattan, the easier it is to use because it has some body and will stand on its own. The very thin has to be spun around an arrangement and hooked on to any strategic spot. The shape used in this design might be called a 'set-piece'. The rattan was soaked in water and when it had become pliable was coaxed into this shape, tied with string and left to dry and 'set'. It is very useful in a number of ways and here I have used it to give rhythm and depth to the base of the design.

These unusual seed-heads might puzzle you. At first glance they appear to be from the iris but they are, in fact, from the tulip. When a friend of mine recently moved into a new house these were in the garden, so naturally I pounced upon them. As all good gardeners cut off the flower heads to prevent plants being debilitated by producing unnecessary seed we do not often see them, and I could not recall having seen them before myself. They are most attractive and as you can see the bottom ones are quite large.

The fan palm (*Tachycarpus fortunei*) can easily be trimmed to any pleasing shape as I have done here. It can also be painted for more dramatic use in show work and sprayed most effectively for your Christmas arrangements.

As you can see from these arrangements I have no qualms at all about using silk flowers. I know that there are some purists who will be horrified at this admission. Mind you, there are silk flowers and silk flowers! The beautifully made and very realistic ones are a godsend to many busy people in the winter months when fresh flowers are so expensive and the warm atmosphere of a centrally heated room soon puts paid to them. I know silk flowers are not cheap but they do last longer—a lifetime if they are treated gently. The 'modern' arranger has an advantage here as she only has to buy them in twos and threes instead of a dozen or so she would need for a traditional arrangement. Sometimes she can even get away with only one, like the delightful branch of blossom used in this design.

I was given this curvaceous piece of fasciated forsythia which fits snugly into one of the openings of this rather unusual pot. The colour of both the wood and the container is reddish-brown which made them an excellent foil for the pink blossom. A great advantage which all these silk flowers have is that their stems are pliable and can be manipulated into whatever shape you desire. It is something I have wished I could do many times with some of our fresh blossom which very often breaks when you are trying to persuade it to your own particular fancy. After inserting the piece of blossom into its allotted place I bent its stem to follow the shape of the wood taking care not to hide any of its beauty.

Once an outline has been made like this it is a simple job to change the flowers now and then so that you do not become bored with having the same arrangement about the house. In fact, it is a good idea to arrange one or two different outlines in your favourite containers as stand-bys so that they can be quickly brought into play when required even at a moment's notice. I find this a very useful device which I can recommend wholeheartedly.

Naturally, for this type of design, outlines would be of dried or glycerined materials which would last indefinitely. Alternatively, such things as basket-cane, rattan, driftwood, bent stalks and plastic waste *et similia* would make possible components for such ideas.

Delightful modern table arrangements can also be made using just a few silk flowers integrating them with a selection of fruit on some sort of platter. For example, various fruits in different shades of green such as avocados, grapes, apples and limes with two or three pink or white carnations on a dark green glass or silver dish would be an attractive combination. An alternative colour scheme could include oranges, satsumas, kiwi fruit, and a selection of nuts in combination with a few glycerined leaves with one or two orange roses set on a bamboo or polished wood base. It is amazing what one can do with a bit of ingenuity and a few carefully chosen items.

When most flower arrangers think of Christmas arrangements thoughts immediately turn to the traditional scene; seldom do they stray in the direction of something in the modern manner. Yet, even with a minimum of materials—provided they are chosen with care—a very evocative Christmas theme can be conjured up.

We have a splendid carved figure of a Madonna and Child in Caen stone by George Thomas which I always like to incorporate into my designs at Christmas time. Its stylized interpretation seems to have an affinity with modern arrangements. It stands about two feet in height and is so dramatic in itself it requires little embellishment. To frame the figure I chose a tall piece of dried palm which I bent and fastened with fine wire to form a halo round the Madonna's head. This was lightly sprayed with gold. At her feet are a group of artificial arum lilies together with a small section of palm leaf. It stood in all its simplicity on a dark brown suede-covered base and when it was spot-lit in my sitting-room it presented quite an impressive sight.

The artificial lilies in this design are plastic and I think many flower arrangers will agree this is the only time of the year that they are acceptable for use in our arrangements. At Christmas time most florists' and club sales tables have a wonderful selection of plastic flowers and foliages in every tint, tone and shade you can think of. Each year the manufacturers seem to choose one specific colour to highlight and full rein is given to every permutation of its variables so you can pretty well tell how long you have had any particular piece! Although these materials have gone up in price over the years they are still a good investment as they last indefinitely. When you get tired of them or when they become a little worse for wear it is a simple job to re-spray them with any colour that takes your fancy. Dried materials, too, which have become a little jaded come into their own again when refreshed with a spot of colour.

For those with nimble fingers all sorts of flowers and foliages can be made at little cost other than one's time. Very realistic carnations can be made with red crepe paper or three-ply dinner napkins and a little dexterity with the pinking shears. A selection of delightful flowers can be made from old nylon tights which have been bleached and dyed pretty colours. Wire petal shapes are formed and the stretch nylon is tightly gathered over them and these in their turn are fastened together to make very attractive flowers. Others can be made with cleverly folded broad ribbons and some 'flowers' I have seen have been simply made using glycerined leaves or honesty discs stuck around open pine cones and sprayed gold. There seems to be no limit to possibilities for home-made 'flowers' and it is great fun experimenting with all kinds of materials to see if you can come up with an original design.

Bibliography

Modern flower arrangement
Aaronson, Marian, *Design with Plant Material*, Grower Books, 1972
Aaronson, Marian, *Flowers in the Modern Manner*, Grower Books, 1981
Brack, Edith, *Flower Arrangement: Free-Style*, Whitethorn Press, 1977
Clements, Julia, *The Art of Arranging a Flower*, B. T. Batsford, 1981
Lim Bian Yam, *The Eye of the Flower Arranger*, W. H. & L. Collingridge, 1967
Reister, Dorothy, *Design for Flower Arrangers*, Van Nostrand Reinhold, 1964
Stockwell, Betty, *Floral Art—Modern and Abstract*, Frederick Warne, 1978
Stratmann, Lyn, *Modern Flower Arranging*, Angus and Robertson, 1979

Plants to grow
Emberton, Sybil, *Garden Foliage for Flower Arrangement*, Faber, 1968
Emberton, Sybil, *Shrub Gardening for Flower Arrangement*, Faber, 1973
Fogg, H. G. Witham, *The Flower Arranger's Garden*, Pelham Books, 1974
Nehrling, Arno & Irene, *Flower Growing for Flower Arrangement*, Dover, 1976
Sackville-West, V, *Garden Book*, Michael Joseph, 1968

Pottery
Casson, Michael, *The Craft of the Potter*, BBC Publications, 1977
Kenny, John B., *Ceramic Design*, Isaac Pitman, 1964
Kenny, John B., *Ceramic Sculpture*, Chilton Book Company, 1967
Rogers, Mary, *On Pottery and Porcelain*, Alphabooks, 1979
Rothenberg, Polly, *The Complete Book of Ceramic Art*, George Allen & Unwin, 1973

Pottery suppliers
Harrison Mayer Ltd., Meir, Stoke-on-Trent, ST3 7PX (who also issue a useful
   quarterly newsletter to customers)
Wengers Ltd., Etruria, Stoke-on-Trent, ST4 7BQ
Podmore & Sons Ltd., Shelton, Stoke-on-Trent

Where to find what

Brack, Edith.
  Modern flower arranging.

0